LIKEABLE RECYCLABLES

CREATIVE IDEAS FOR REUSING BAGS, BOXES, CANS, AND CARTONS

WRITTEN BY LINDA SCHWARTZ • ILLUSTRATED BY BEV ARMSTRONG

The Learning Works

Cover Design & Illustration:
Beverly Armstrong

Text Design & Editorial Production:
Sherri M. Butterfield

The Learning Works, Inc.
P.O. Box 6187
Santa Barbara, California   93160

Library of Congress Catalog Card Number: 92-81436
ISBN 0-88160-210-8

Printed in the United States of America. Current Printing (last digit): 10 9 8 7 6 5 4 3 2

Introduction

Garbage is a growing problem in our world. Only about 10 percent of the waste material we produce is recycled. A whopping 80 percent of this material finds its way into landfills. At this rate, half of this country's landfills will be full by the year 2000.

What can we do to solve this problem? We can reduce the amount of garbage we produce by purchasing wisely, by reusing regularly, and by recycling more materials more often.

Likeable Recyclables offers an endless array of fun-filled ways to keep bottles, boxes, cans, cartons, cups, tubes, and other discards from finding their way into overcrowded landfills by transforming them into toys, games, and other objects to keep, use, and enjoy.

This book makes it easy to turn trash into treasure. By following its whimsically illustrated instructions, you can do something fun for yourself and something good for the earth.

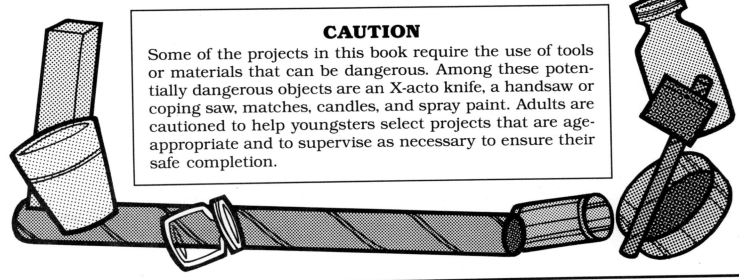

CAUTION

Some of the projects in this book require the use of tools or materials that can be dangerous. Among these potentially dangerous objects are an X-acto knife, a handsaw or coping saw, matches, candles, and spray paint. Adults are cautioned to help youngsters select projects that are age-appropriate and to supervise as necessary to ensure their safe completion.

Contents

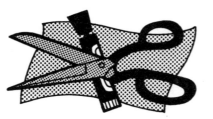

Contents
(continued)

BOTTLES & CANS, 59-92

Contents
(continued)

BAGS, CUPS, TUBES & MORE, 93-128

TIPS
&
TOOLS

Odds and Ends Collection

Below is a list of things you may want to save, recycle,
and reuse for the projects described in this book.

- ☐ aluminum foil
- ☐ beads
- ☐ bottle caps
- ☐ brads
- ☐ burlap
- ☐ buttons
- ☐ cans
- ☐ cardboard tubes
- ☐ carpet samples
- ☐ computer paper
- ☐ corks
- ☐ cotton balls

- ☐ drinking straws
- ☐ egg cartons
- ☐ fabric scraps
- ☐ feathers
- ☐ felt
- ☐ film canisters
- ☐ food trays
- ☐ greeting cards
- ☐ ice cream sticks
- ☐ jar lids
- ☐ lace
- ☐ leather scraps

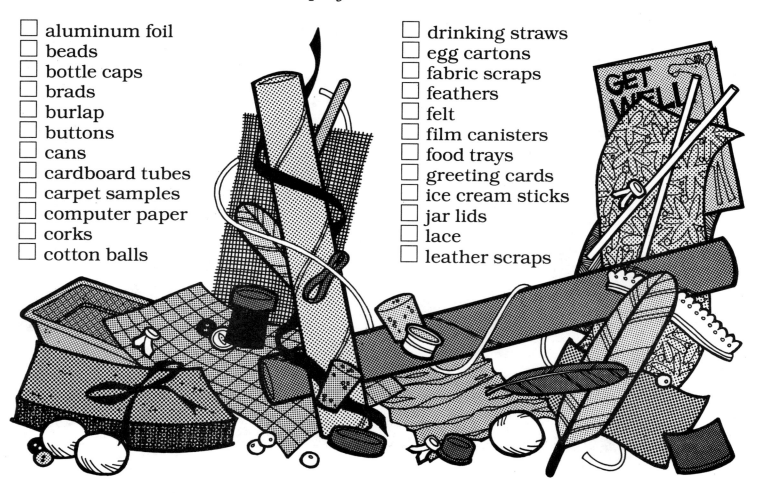

Odds and Ends Collection
(continued)

- [ ] magazines
- [ ] margarine tubs
- [ ] milk cartons
- [ ] nails
- [ ] newspapers
- [ ] paper, colored and plain
- [ ] paper clips
- [ ] paper cups
- [ ] paper plates
- [ ] pasta, dry
- [ ] pie tins
- [ ] pipe cleaners
- [ ] pizza boxes
- [ ] ribbon

- [ ] shells
- [ ] sponges
- [ ] spools
- [ ] stamps, canceled
- [ ] string
- [ ] tissue paper
- [ ] toothpicks
- [ ] twine
- [ ] wallpaper scraps
- [ ] wire
- [ ] wire hangers
- [ ] wood scraps
- [ ] wrapping paper
- [ ] yarn

Tools and Materials

Below is a list of some of the tools and materials you may need to complete the projects described in this book. Before beginning any project, check to see what you will need, and be sure that you have all of the necessary tools and materials on hand.

- [ ] acrylic polymer medium
- [ ] candles, household
- [ ] can opener, punch type
- [ ] cardboard, thick and/or corrugated
- [ ] chalk
- [ ] coat hangers, wire
- [ ] crayons
- [ ] dowels
- [ ] elastic strips
- [ ] envelopes, large
- [ ] glue, white
- [ ] hammer
- [ ] handsaw

- [ ] hole punch, single hole
- [ ] imagination
- [ ] knife, pocket or paring
- [ ] line, laundry
- [ ] line, nylon fish
- [ ] marbles
- [ ] measuring cups
- [ ] mirrors, purse size
- [ ] needle and thread
- [ ] paint, gold or silver spray
- [ ] paint, tempera
- [ ] paintbrushes
- [ ] panty hose

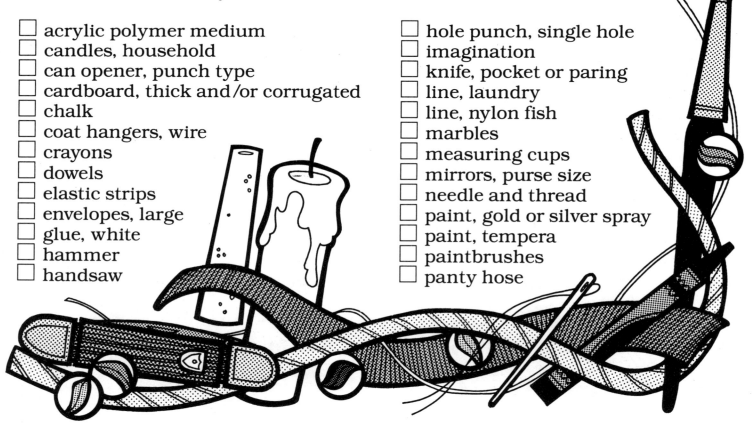

Tools and Materials
(continued)

- ☐ particle board
- ☐ pencils, sharpened and unsharpened
- ☐ pens, felt-tipped
- ☐ pens, permanent marking
- ☐ pins, straight
- ☐ pliers
- ☐ popcorn, unpopped
- ☐ rice, uncooked
- ☐ rolling pin
- ☐ rope, lightweight
- ☐ rubber bands
- ☐ ruler
- ☐ salt
- ☐ sand
- ☐ saw, coping
- ☐ scissors, fabric
- ☐ scissors, paper
- ☐ seeds

- ☐ self-adhesive dots, spots, circles, strips, and/or labels
- ☐ socks
- ☐ soil, potting
- ☐ stapler with staples
- ☐ starch, liquid
- ☐ stickers, decorative
- ☐ tape, adhesive
- ☐ tape, cellophane
- ☐ tape, duct
- ☐ tape, masking
- ☐ tape measure
- ☐ towel, absorbent terry cloth
- ☐ towels, paper
- ☐ twist ties
- ☐ varnish
- ☐ varnish thinner
- ☐ wire cutters
- ☐ X-acto knife

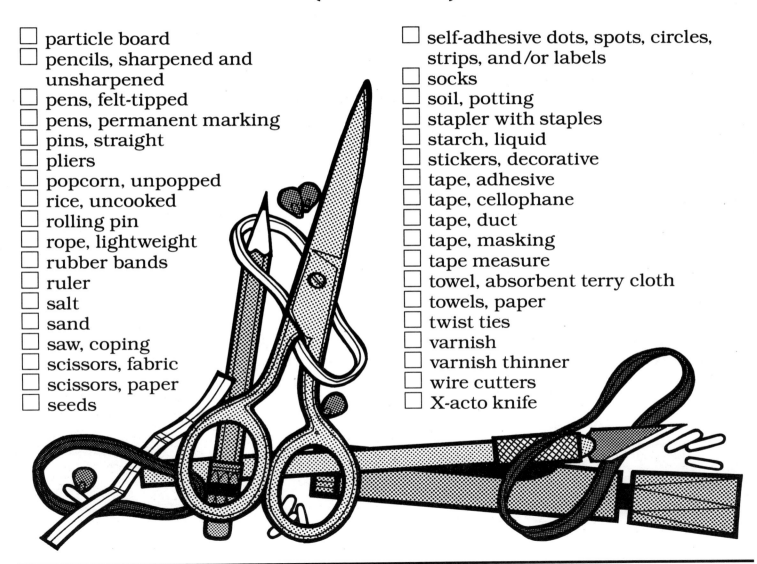

How to Cover a Box

WHAT YOU NEED

- ☐ a box
- ☐ a pencil
- ☐ a small sheet of paper
- ☐ a ruler (if your box is small)
- ☐ a meter stick (if your box is large)
- ☐ some butcher paper, shelf paper, construction paper, or gift wrap
- ☐ a pair of scissors
- ☐ some tape or glue

ONE WAY TO DO IT

1. Using the ruler or meter stick, measure each of the six sides of the box.
2. Write down these measurements on the small piece of paper.
3. Using the pencil and the ruler or the meter stick, draw six rectangles on the large sheet of paper to match these measurements.
4. Carefully cut out these rectangles.
5. Glue each rectangle to the appropriate side of the box.

ANOTHER WAY TO DO IT

1. Place the box on the sheet of paper.
2. Wrap the paper loosely around the box to be certain that the paper is large enough to cover the box.
3. Wrap the paper tightly around the sides of the box, overlapping the edges of the paper, and tape or glue the seam shut.
4. To finish one end, carefully fold the paper in at the sides.
5. Fold the bottom flap up, fold the top flap down, and tape or glue it to the bottom flap or to the bottom of the box.
6. Repeat steps 4 and 5 for the other end of the box.

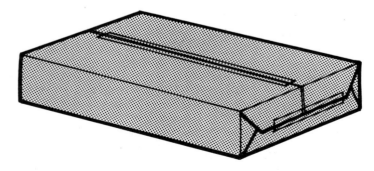

How to Cover a Tube

WHAT YOU NEED

☐ a cardboard tube
☐ a pencil
☐ a ruler and a tape measure
☐ some colored or patterned paper
☐ a pair of scissors
☐ some tape or glue
☐ two self-adhesive circles (optional)

ONE WAY TO DO IT

1. Using the ruler, measure the height of the tube and write down this measurement.
2. With the tape measure, measure the circumference of the tube and write down this measurement.
3. Using the pencil and ruler, carefully draw a rectangle on the paper which is 2 inches higher than the height of the tube and 1/2 inch wider than the circumference of the tube.
4. Wrap the paper rectangle around the tube and tape or glue the seam.
5. Carefully fold the paper in at each

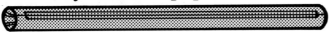

end and tape it in place or cover it with a self-adhesive circle.

ANOTHER WAY TO DO IT

1. Follow steps 1 and 2 above.
2. Using the pencil and ruler, carefully draw a rectangle on the paper which is *exactly* as high as the tube and 1/2 inch wider than the circumference of the tube.
3. Wrap the paper around the tube and tape or glue the seam closed.
4. Measure the diameter of the opening in the end of the tube and cut two circles whose diameter is one inch larger than this diameter.
5. "Fringe" each circle by making a series of cuts about 1/4 inch apart and about 1/2 inch long from the outside of the circle toward the center.
6. Place one circle on each end of the tube, fold down the fringe, and glue the fringe to the sides of the tube to hold the circle in place.

Recipe for
Papier-Mâché Mixture

WHAT YOU NEED

- [ ] one large mixing bowl
- [ ] a measuring cup
- [ ] 2 cups of flour
- [ ] 6 cups of water
- [ ] a spoon
- [ ] some newspapers, paper towels, or other pulpy paper torn into strips about an inch wide and 6 inches long

WHAT YOU DO

1. Put two cups of flour in a large mixing bowl.
2. Add 6 cups of water.
3. With the spoon, stir the flour-and-water mixture until it is smooth and pasty.
4. To apply the mixture, either pull the paper strips through it or paint it on with a brush.
5. Allow each layer of wet paper strips to dry thoroughly before you add another layer.

BOXES

Cereal Box Kangaroo

WHAT YOU NEED

- [ ] one large cereal box
- [ ] a smaller box for the pouch
- [ ] a tiny box for the baby kangaroo
- [ ] a pair of scissors
- [ ] a paper cup
- [ ] a black felt-tipped marking pen
- [ ] construction paper and/or cardboard
- [ ] tape and/or glue

WHAT YOU DO

1. Cut all three boxes down one side and around three sides of each end.
2. Invert the boxes so that the plain gray or brown cardboard faces out.
3. Tape the boxes back together.
4. Attach the smaller box to the front of the large one.
5. Add a paper cup nose.
6. Cut ears, feet, and tail from colored paper, cardboard, or another empty cereal box and attach them as shown.
7. Use the pen to add eyes, mouth, and other details.
8. Turn the tiny box into a baby kangaroo and put it in the mother's pouch.

Puzzle Time

Create a puzzle from recycled cereal boxes. Make it as easy or as hard as you wish.

WHAT YOU NEED

☐ two identical large cereal boxes
☐ a pencil
☐ a pair of sharp scissors
☐ one envelope, a little larger than the cereal box front
☐ glue

WHAT YOU DO

1. Cut the fronts off both cereal boxes.
2. Using the pencil, draw a puzzle pattern on the plain side of one box front.
3. With the scissors, carefully cut along the lines you have drawn to separate the puzzle pieces.
4. Glue the uncut cereal box front to the large envelope.
5. Store the puzzle pieces in the envelope when they are not in use.
6. Have fun working the puzzle yourself or challenge a friend to give it a try.

Toothpaste Box Monsters

Make a monster from recycled toothpaste boxes. It can be as fearsome, fantastic, or friendly as you like.

WHAT YOU NEED

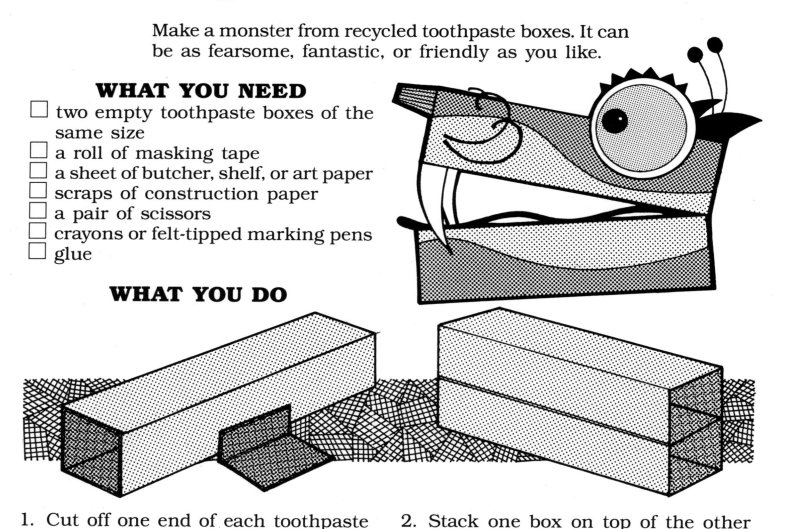

- [ ] two empty toothpaste boxes of the same size
- [ ] a roll of masking tape
- [ ] a sheet of butcher, shelf, or art paper
- [ ] scraps of construction paper
- [ ] a pair of scissors
- [ ] crayons or felt-tipped marking pens
- [ ] glue

WHAT YOU DO

1. Cut off one end of each toothpaste box.

2. Stack one box on top of the other with the open ends together.

Toothpaste Box Monsters
(continued)

3. Use a strip of masking tape to hinge the boxes together at the open ends as shown.

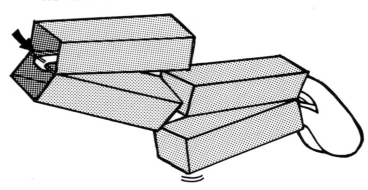

4. Add monster features, including ears, eyes, fangs, and horns.

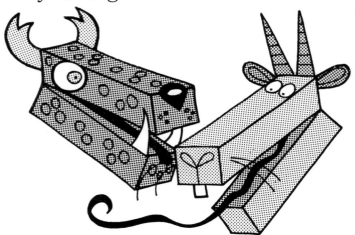

5. Draw, color, cut out, and attach a paper body to this head.

A Perfect Puppet Partner

WHAT YOU NEED

- [ ] one large detergent or cereal box
- [ ] large scraps of cloth or paper with which you can cover the box and from which you can cut arms and legs
- [ ] a paper plate
- [ ] one pair of shoelaces or two pieces of cord 2 feet long
- [ ] four big rubber bands
- [ ] a pair of scissors
- [ ] a pencil and crayons, paint, or pens
- [ ] a stapler with staples
- [ ] glue
- [ ] assorted objects from your odds and ends collection

WHAT YOU DO

1. Cover the front, sides, and back of the box with cloth or paper.
2. Draw a face on the paper plate.
3. Glue the plate to the box as shown.
4. For the puppet's arms, cut two strips of cloth about 3 inches wide and 6 inches longer than your arms.
5. For the puppet's legs, cut two strips of cloth about 3 inches wide and 6 inches longer than your legs.

A Perfect Puppet Partner
(continued)

6. Glue the arms and legs to the back of the box.

7. Loop the end of each arm through a rubber band and staple as shown.
8. Similarly loop the end of each leg through a rubber band and staple.

9. Punch two holes in the top and two holes in the back of the box.
10. Tie one shoelace or piece of cord through each set of holes. Leave enough string to tie behind your neck.

11. To wear your puppet, tie the shoelaces or cord loosely around your neck. Put the rubber bands around your wrists and ankles. Make your puppet partner move.

Puppet Pop-ups

WHAT YOU NEED

- [ ] one large, empty cereal box for the head
- [ ] a sheet of colored construction paper for the face
- [ ] scraps of construction paper in assorted colors for the features
- [ ] crayons or felt-tipped marking pens
- [ ] a pair of sharp scissors
- [ ] glue
- [ ] a stick about 18 inches long
- [ ] tape
- [ ] accessories such as an old top hat, a baseball cap, or a cowboy hat, and a necktie, a muffler, or a kerchief

WHAT YOU DO

1. Cover the front of the cereal box with paper.
2. Use crayons or marking pens to draw eyes, nose, mustache, and chin on the paper or cut these features from bits of colored construction paper and attach them with glue.

Puppet Pop-ups
(continued)

3. Using sharp scissors, cut around the box between the mustache and the chin, where the mouth should be.

4. Glue or tape one end of the stick inside the top part of the box.

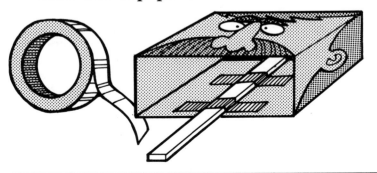

5. Cut a hole in the bottom part of the box and slide the stick through it.

6. To give your puppet pop-up more character, add a baseball cap, a cowboy hat, or a top hat and a kerchief, a muffler, or a necktie.

7. Hold the bottom of the box with one hand and move the stick up and down with the other hand to make your puppet talk.

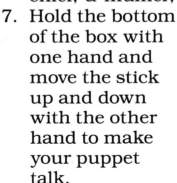

Puppet Stage

WHAT YOU NEED

- ☐ one empty cardboard box of the kind used for large appliances like refrigerators, washing machines, or big-screen television sets
- ☐ an X-acto knife
- ☐ leftover interior latex (water-base) paint
- ☐ a paintbrush
- ☐ enough fabric from your odds and ends collection to make a small curtain
- ☐ a pair of pinking shears or other fabric scissors
- ☐ tape or thumb tacks to use in attaching the curtain to the box

WHAT YOU DO

1. Cut off the back panel of the box.
2. Cut a window in the front panel of the box.
3. Paint the top, front, and sides of the box.
4. Cut curtains from the fabric and hang, tape, or tack them in the window.

Periscope Peeker

A **periscope** is a tube that enables those who use it to see over obstacles and around corners. Mirrors carefully arranged inside the tube "reposition" objects that are "invisible," by means of reflection, for convenient viewing. You can fashion your own periscope peeker from an empty cardboard box.

WHAT YOU NEED

- [ ] one empty cardboard box from a roll of food wrap or aluminum foil
- [ ] pencil and paper
- [ ] a ruler
- [ ] a pair of sharp scissors
- [ ] a coping saw (optional)
- [ ] a piece of shirt cardboard or a tablet back
- [ ] two small cosmetic or purse mirrors measuring about 1-7/8 inches by 2-3/4 inches
- [ ] some white glue
- [ ] a roll of masking or mending tape

WHAT YOU DO

1. If your box has a metal cutting strip along one edge, use scissors to trim off this strip, being careful to remove as little of the cardboard as possible.

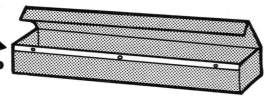

metal cutting strip

Periscope Peeker
(continued)

2. Carefully cut a 2-inch square window in the top of the box near one end, leaving a 1/2-inch strip of cardboard on the end.

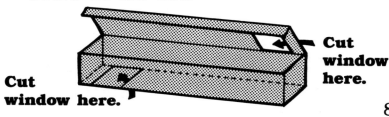

Cut window here.

Cut window here.

3. Cut a 2-inch square window in the bottom of the box near the other end, again leaving a 1/2-inch strip of cardboard on the end.
4. Glue the box shut and allow the glue to dry.
5. Lay the box on its side.
6. Using the pencil and ruler, measure the height of the box at the end and write down this measurement.

7. Measure along one side of the box, from the end toward the middle, and place a mark where this measurement is the same as the height of the box.

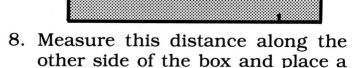

8. Measure this distance along the other side of the box and place a mark.
9. Using the pencil and the ruler, draw a straight line across the box connecting these marks.

10. Now draw a line that extends diagonally across the square you have made at the end of the box.

Periscope Peeker
(continued)

11. With the scissors or the saw, cut along this diagonal line and slice off the end of the box.

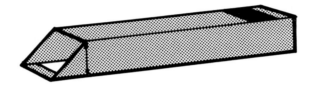

12. Repeat steps 6 through 11 for the other end of the box.

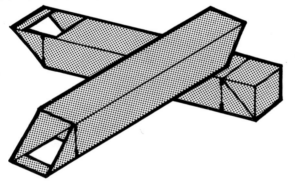

13. Using the ruler, measure the open ends of the box.

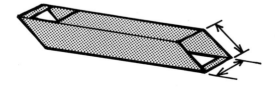

14. Cut two pieces of cardboard to match these measurements and to cover and close both ends of the box.

15. Glue one mirror in the center of each piece of cardboard.

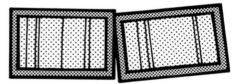

16. Tape one cardboard piece to each end of the box with the mirror facing inside the box.

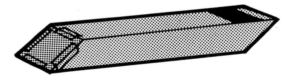

17. Hold your periscope peeker so that you can peer into one window and out the other.
18. Enjoy what you see.

Create a Vehicle

Using scissors and your imagination, turn an empty shoe box into a dream vehicle.

WHAT YOU NEED

- one empty shoe box
- several smaller boxes in assorted sizes and shapes
- two round, unsharpened pencils to serve as axles
- eight rubber bands
- stiff, thick cardboard for wheels
- a pencil
- a pair of sharp scissors
- a hole punch
- a roll of masking tape
- felt-tipped marking pens
- colored construction paper
- aluminum foil

WHAT YOU DO

1. Remove the box lid and save it for later use as a hood, trunk lid, convertible top, or cab cover.
2. Use scissors to shape the sides of the box to fit the design you have in mind.

Create a Vehicle
(continued)

3. Tape the unsharpened pencils securely to the bottom of the shoe box to serve as axles.

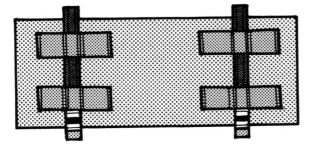

4. Cut four round wheels the same size from stiff, thick cardboard.
5. Punch or cut a hole in the center of each wheel.

6. Wrap a rubber band around each end of each axle.
7. Put the wheels on the axles.
8. Wrap a rubber band around each end of each axle to hold the cardboard wheels in place.

9. Use the smaller boxes, marking pens, and foil or paper scraps to add seats, doors, windows, headlights, and other features.

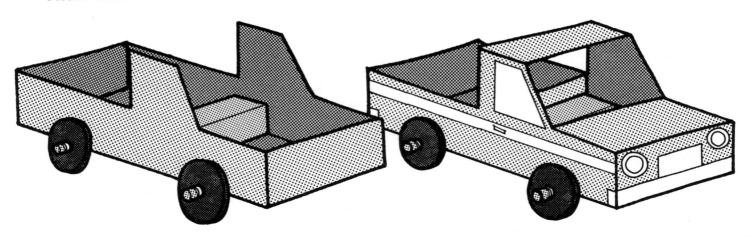

All-About-Me Cube

Use pictures and slogans that you draw, write, or cut from old magazines to represent your likes, dislikes, hobbies, pets, memories from the past, plans for the future, and more.

WHAT YOU NEED

- [ ] one empty cardboard box
- [ ] some butcher, shelf, or other colored paper
- [ ] a pair of scissors
- [ ] a roll of tape
- [ ] some glue
- [ ] several old magazines
- [ ] felt-tipped marking pens in assorted colors

WHAT YOU DO

1. Cover the box with colored paper. (For instructions, see page 12.)
2. Decorate the box with pictures and slogans that you draw, write, or cut from old magazines.
3. Display your All-About-Me Cube for others to enjoy.

Pasta Packages

This container makes an ideal gift and will hold paper clips, rubber bands, jewelry, safety pins, or loose change.

WHAT YOU NEED

- ☐ one small box or margarine tub with a lid
- ☐ fancy dry pasta, such as bows, twists, and/or shells
- ☐ gold or silver spray paint
- ☐ ribbon, rick-rack, or yarn
- ☐ glue

WHAT YOU DO

1. Glue the pasta to the top of the lid.
2. Allow plenty of time for the glue to dry.
3. Spray both the container and the lid with gold or silver paint.
4. Glue ribbon, rick-rack, or yarn around the edge of the lid.

CAUTION

Spray paint can be both messy and dangerous. Before you use it, read the warnings on the label. Work in an area that is well ventilated. Spread out plenty of old newspapers to protect the floor and walls in this area. Shake the can well before spraying. Aim the nozzle carefully so that the paint will go where you want it to go and *not* toward your face or into your eyes.

Design a Dollhouse

WHAT YOU NEED

- [ ] four or more empty medium-sized cartons or shoe boxes for the rooms in the house
- [ ] some smaller boxes for furniture
- [ ] tape or glue
- [ ] a pair of sharp scissors
- [ ] carpet and fabric scraps
- [ ] construction paper or wallpaper scraps
- [ ] additional things from your odds and ends collection

WHAT YOU DO

1. Arrange the boxes side by side or stack them one atop another.
2. Attach the boxes together with tape.

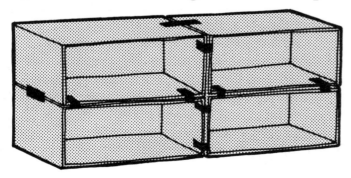

3. Color and decorate the outsides of the boxes to look like the outside of a house. Draw windows and doors. Add flowers and shrubs cut from colored construction paper.

Design a Dollhouse
(continued)

4. Color and decorate the insides of the boxes to look like the rooms in a house. Use carpet, fabric, and wallpaper scraps from your odds and ends collection. Add curtains and drapes.

5. To furnish these rooms, use chairs, tables, and beds you have made from empty matchboxes and spools, and from scraps of wood. Add quilts and coverlets, bedspreads and tablecloths cut from fabric scraps.

Create a Castle

WHAT YOU NEED

- [ ] an assortment of empty boxes, tubes, and cartons to be used for castle rooms and towers
- [ ] a piece of heavy brown paper or lightweight cardboard, or one large, flat side from an empty box
- [ ] construction paper in such colors as gray or tan and red, blue, or green to cover the walls and to make the peaked roofs and pennants
- [ ] a pair of scissors
- [ ] tape and glue
- [ ] felt-tipped marking pens
- [ ] several toothpicks
- [ ] a paper punch
- [ ] some string
- [ ] a piece of stiff cardboard, particle board, or wood to be used as a base

ALL ABOUT CASTLES

In medieval times, there were castles. At first, they were little more than sturdy houses surrounded by high fences. These structures were simple strongholds, or **fortresses**, designed to protect the people who lived in them or sought refuge behind their walls.

Create a Castle
(continued)

ALL ABOUT CASTLES

As time passed, castles were made larger and more elaborate. The lords who lived in them built stone towers, called **keeps** or **donjons**. Sometimes, they placed slanted foundations, called **plinths**, at the bases of the keeps to strengthen them.

Around the tops of the keeps, they added **battlements**. These structures were walls with high places to hide behind in the event of an attack and low places to look and shoot through during battle. The high places were called **merlons**, and the low places were called **crenels**.

Atop the peaked tower roofs, **pennants** and **banners** fluttered in the breeze and told passersby when the noble lord of the castle was in residence. Inside, **gonfalons** and **tapestries** were hung from beams and rafters to beautify the gray stone walls and to block the wind that found its way through the many cracks in them.

WHAT YOU DO

1. Cover each box with brown or tan construction paper.

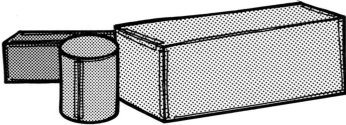

2. Draw and/or cut out windows in the castle towers.
3. Use the marking pens to give the walls the uneven texture of stacked stone.

Create a Castle
(continued)

4. For peaked tower roofs, cut semicircles from red, blue, or green construction paper.
5. Roll these paper semicircles into cones large enough to fit over the tops of the tubes.
6. Glue or tape the straight sides together.

7. To make pennants, cut triangles from bright-colored paper.
8. Apply a small amount of glue to the short side of each triangle and fold it over a toothpick so that the glue is on the inside.
9. Insert the toothpicks into the roof cones and secure them with glue or tape.

10. Select a box to be the front of your castle and to hold the drawbridge.
11. To make a drawbridge for your castle, cut a rectangle from a piece of lightweight cardboard, heavy brown paper, or one side of an empty box.
12. Punch holes in two corners of this rectangle.
13. Run string through each hole and tie it, leaving a long, loose end.

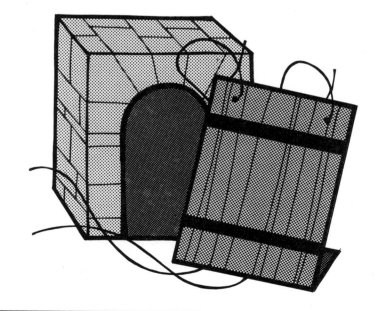

Create a Castle
(continued)

14. Fold the bottom edge of the rectangle back and glue it to the bottom of this box.

15. Punch holes in the front of this box.
16. Put the loose end of one piece of string through each hole in the box and knot the string inside the box so that it can be pulled and released.

17. Arrange the rooms and towers of your castle on a base made from a flat piece of stiff cardboard, particle board, or wood.

Observation Station

WHAT YOU NEED

☐ an empty pint- or quart-sized milk carton
☐ a pair of sharp scissors
☐ one leg from an old pair of panty hose
☐ a small rubber band

WHAT YOU DO

To prepare your observation station

1. Cut off the top of the milk carton.
2. Lay the milk carton on one side.
3. Cut at least one viewing window in each of the other three sides.
4. Put the carton into the foot of the panty hose.
5. Cut off the panty hose leg about 4 inches above the top of the carton.
6. Wrap the rubber band around the top of the panty hose leg to close it tightly.

To find an insect to observe

7. Remove the rubber band from the top of the panty hose leg.
8. Go outside and find a friendly insect you might like to observe.
9. Catch the insect gently.
10. Carefully place the insect in your observation station.
11. Add a twig, a leaf, or some grass for the insect to crawl on.
12. Pull the panty hose snugly around the carton and wrap the rubber band tightly around the open end.
13. Watch the insect for a while. How many legs does it have? Does it have wings? If so, how many? Where are its eyes? How does it move? Does it crawl, walk, hop, or fly?
14. Before nightfall, take the insect back to where you found it and let it go.

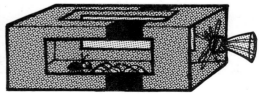

Make a Gator

WHAT YOU NEED

- [ ] two empty egg cartons
- [ ] a pair of scissors
- [ ] a pencil
- [ ] eight garbage bag twist ties
- [ ] one marking pen
- [ ] some white construction paper
- [ ] tape or glue

WHAT YOU DO

1. To make the head of your gator, cut across one egg carton to separate a square block of four egg cups from the remaining eight.

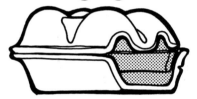

2. Trim off the sides and edges of this four-cup section.

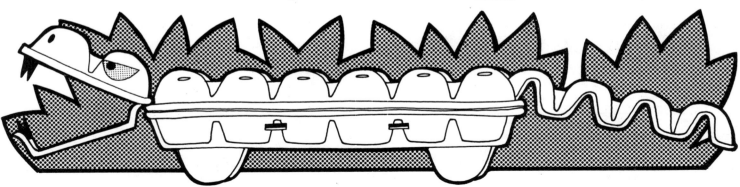

Make a Gator
(continued)

3. With the pencil point, poke four holes in this four-cup section as shown.

4. To make the body of your gator, turn the uncut egg carton so that the flat cover is down. Use the pencil to poke four holes in one end of this carton to match the four holes you poked in the head.

5. Open the carton. Bend one garbage bag twist tie in the middle and slide the ends through two of the holes in the head.

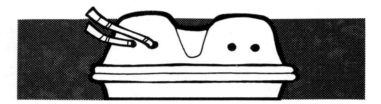

6. Push the ends of the tie through two of the holes in the body and twist these ends together inside the body.
7. Repeat this process for the other two holes in the head and body.

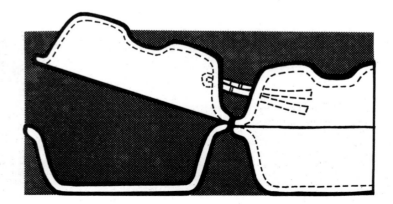

Make a Gator
(continued)

8. To make the tail of your gator, cut straight down the middle of the eight remaining egg cups and trim the edges from one set of four.

9. Use the pencil to poke two holes in one end of the tail.
10. Poke two holes in the tail end of the body to match the two holes you poked in the tail.
11. To attach the tail to the body, loop one garbage twist tie through the two holes in the tail.
12. Push the loose tie ends through the two body holes and twist these ends together inside the body.

13. To add legs, on the flat cover of the body, poke two holes near each corner.
14. Cut apart the four remaining egg cups and trim the edges. Use one cup for each leg.

15. Poke two holes in the bottom of each cup.
16. Loop one tie through each leg and into two body holes.
17. Twist the tie ends together inside the body.
18. To give your gator some personality, use a marking pen to add eyes on the head. Cut teeth from construction paper and tape or glue them into the mouth.

Construct a City

WHAT YOU NEED

- [ ] an assortment of empty boxes, tubes, and cartons to be used for various city buildings and features
- [ ] a large piece of stiff cardboard, particle board, or wood to be used as a base
- [ ] construction paper in such colors as brown, gray, or tan and red, blue, or green to cover building walls, make roofs, and add shrubs and trees
- [ ] a pair of sharp scissors
- [ ] tape or glue
- [ ] felt-tipped marking pens

WHAT YOU DO

1. Plan your city before you begin. Decide which ones of the following buildings you will include and where you will place each one.

apartments	libraries
banks	movie theaters
department stores	museums
fire stations	office buildings
gas stations	police stations
grocery stores	post offices
hospitals	restaurants
houses	schools

Construct a City
(continued)

2. Cover the boxes with construction paper to hide their decorations and labels.
3. Use marking pens or shapes cut from construction paper to add doors, windows, porches, stairs, columns, and other architectural elements to the fronts and sides of the covered boxes.

4. Where appropriate, "paint" signs and labels on these buildings.
5. Arrange your city buildings on the base.
6. Add sidewalks, streets, people, cars, trees, and other special features to make your city seem real.

Decorate a Box for Paper

WHAT YOU NEED

- [ ] a large cereal box
- [ ] recycled gift wrap or brown paper cut from a grocery sack
- [ ] a pair of scissors
- [ ] felt-tipped marking pens
- [ ] tape and glue

WHAT YOU DO

1. Cover the box with the paper, carefully taping the ends in place.
2. Label the box by cutting letters from paper scraps and gluing them to the box or by writing letters on the box with felt-tipped marking pens.
3. Decorate the box by drawing on it and/or by gluing paper shapes to it.
4. Use the box to hold art paper, computer paper, and/or writing paper that has been used only on one side and is still clean on the other side.
5. When you need paper for a first draft, rough sketch, or shopping list, take a sheet from this decorated and decorative box.

VARIATION

Similarly decorate two larger cardboard boxes. Use one to store newspapers and the other to store nonglossy assorted paper that you cannot reuse but can recycle.

Pudding People

WHAT YOU NEED

- [ ] an empty pudding or gelatin box for each pudding person you wish to make
- [ ] colored construction paper
- [ ] felt-tipped marking pens
- [ ] a pair of sharply pointed scissors
- [ ] tape and glue
- [ ] things from your odds and ends collection
- [ ] one tongue depressor or recycled ice cream stick for each pudding person

WHAT YOU DO

1. Cover a box with construction paper.
2. Using felt-tipped pens, shapes cut from construction paper, and/or things from your odds and ends collection, add eyes, nose, mouth, ears, some hair, and a hat or a cap.
3. To add a handle, use scissors to make a slit in the bottom of the box.
4. Slide an ice cream stick up through this slit.
5. If the stick pulls out easily, tape or glue it securely in place.

Cartoon Capers

WHAT YOU NEED

- a large cardboard box
- a pair of sharp scissors
- a roll of white shelf paper
- two cardboard tubes or wooden dowels that are slightly taller than your box
- some masking tape
- a ruler
- felt-tipped marking pens in assorted colors

WHAT YOU DO

1. Set the box on its side so that the open top becomes the back.
2. To make the screen, cut a large rectangle in the front of the box. This rectangle should be no taller than the roll of white paper.
3. Choose an environmental theme that interests you, such as conserving water, enjoying nature, helping endangered wildlife, reusing and recycling, saving energy, and stopping pollution.

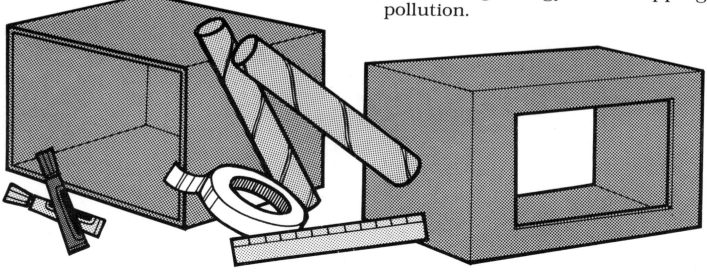

Cartoon Capers
(continued)

4. Create a cartoon strip based on this theme. Draw and color a series of pictures on the roll of paper. Use the ruler to make each picture frame *slightly larger* than your screen.
5. With the scissors, cut two holes in the top of the box and two holes in the bottom of the box, in the corners and near the screen.
6. Insert the ends of the tubes or dowels into the holes.

7. Tape each end of your completed cartoon strip around a tube or dowel.
8. Set the box at the edge of a desk or table so that the dowels can turn freely.
9. To view your cartoon strip, slowly turn the dowels.
10. To rewind for another showing, turn the dowels in the other direction.

A Tiny Treasure Chest

WHAT YOU NEED

- [ ] a small, empty cardboard or wooden box with a top or lid
- [ ] some old magazines with plenty of words and pictures
- [ ] a pair of scissors
- [ ] white glue
- [ ] several paintbrushes
- [ ] varnish
- [ ] varnish thinner
- [ ] a square or two of felt

WHAT YOU DO

1. Choose a theme for your treasure chest.
2. Look through old magazines to find words and pictures that fit this theme, and cut them out.
3. Arrange the words and pictures in a pleasing pattern on the top, bottom, and sides of the box so that their edges overlap.
4. Glue the words and pictures in place, and allow the glue to dry.
5. Brush a thin coat of varnish evenly over the words and pictures, and allow it to dry.
6. Brush on a second coat of varnish.
7. While this varnish is drying, soak your paintbrush in varnish thinner and clean it well.
8. Line the inside of the box with felt to give it a finished look.
9. Loosely hinge the top of the box to the bottom of the box with felt strips.
10. Glue a felt tab or loop to the box lid to serve as a handle.
11. Use this chest to store jewelry or other special treasures.

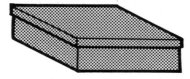
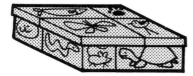
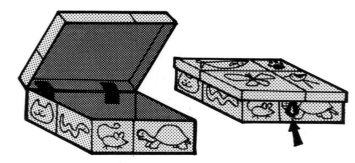

Shoe Box Peek Show

WHAT YOU NEED

- [ ] one shoe box with lid
- [ ] some colored shelf paper or a sheet of gift wrap
- [ ] felt-tipped marking pens in assorted colors
- [ ] pictures cut from magazines
- [ ] scraps of construction paper
- [ ] pieces of cardboard or tag board
- [ ] a pair of scissors and/or an X-acto knife
- [ ] things from your odds and ends collection
- [ ] some tape or glue

WHAT YOU DO

1. Remove the lid from the shoe box.
2. Cover the lid with shelf paper or gift wrap.
3. Cut a 2-inch square window in the lid for light.

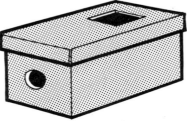

4. Wrap the box with shelf paper or gift wrap. If this paper is plain, use marking pens to add shapes and colors.
5. Cut a small hole in one end of your box to peek through.
6. Choose a theme, such as a holiday, a historical event, a movie you have seen, or a book you have read.
7. Based on this theme, create a three-dimensional scene inside the box, facing the hole at the end. Draw and/or cut out the shapes you need. Tape or glue some of these shapes to the sides of the box. Stand other shapes in the middle of the box.
8. Put the lid back on the box.
9. Look through the hole to enjoy the scene inside the box. Invite others to take a peek.

Shoe Box Dragon

WHAT YOU NEED

- [ ] an empty shoe box with lid
- [ ] a pair of scissors
- [ ] a stapler and staples
- [ ] some masking tape
- [ ] a thick rubber band
- [ ] felt-tipped marking pens
- [ ] scraps of paper and/or fabric
- [ ] things from your odds and ends collection
- [ ] some glue

WHAT YOU DO

1. Cut the corners on one end of a shoe box lid and lift the flap.

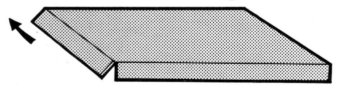

2. Staple a rubber band to the top of the lid, near the flap, as shown.

3. Use masking tape to attach the lid flap to one end of the box.

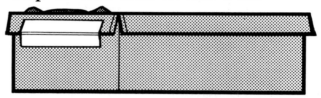

4. Use marking pens to draw eyes, teeth, and a tongue on the box, or cut appropriate shapes from scraps of paper or fabric and glue them to it.

5. Putting your fingers under the rubber band and resting your thumb against the end of the box, move the lid up and down to open and close your shoe box dragon's mouth.

Egg Cup Bouquets

Recycle empty egg cartons into fancy floral bouquets.

WHAT YOU NEED

- [ ] several egg cartons made of aqua, yellow, or some other pastel shade of polystyrene foam
- [ ] a pair of sharp scissors
- [ ] a sharpened pencil
- [ ] some pipe cleaners
- [ ] ribbon and/or a narrow-necked vase

WHAT YOU DO

1. With scissors, cut the egg cartons into single egg cups.

2. To make these egg cups look like flowers, fringe, point, and scallop them as shown.

3. Using the point of the pencil or scissors, carefully poke a small hole in the center of each egg cup.
4. Insert a pipe cleaner in the hole.
5. Bend the end of the pipe cleaner to hold it in place.
6. Tie the stems of your egg carton bouquet together with ribbon or place them in a narrow-necked vase.

VARIATION

Cut several egg cups to different heights and layer them together on the same pipe cleaner stem.

Shoe Box Choo-Choose

Turn four empty shoe boxes into a picture-sorting activity for young children.

WHAT YOU NEED

- [ ] four empty shoe boxes without lids
- [ ] some old magazines
- [ ] cardboard or tag board for wheels
- [ ] scraps of construction paper
- [ ] a pair of sharp scissors
- [ ] a large envelope to hold the magazine pictures
- [ ] some glue
- [ ] string or yarn

WHAT YOU DO

1. To turn the boxes into cars, cut sixteen round cardboard wheels and glue four to each box. Use shapes cut from construction paper, cardboard, tag board, or the shoe box lids to add a cab and cowcatcher to the engine.
2. Connect the cars to make a train. Glue string or yarn to the ends of the boxes or punch holes in the box ends, push the string or yarn through, and knot it.

Shoe Box Choo-Choose
(continued)

3. Choose four categories, one for each train car. For example, you might choose the four food groups: (1) meat and fish, (2) fruits and vegetables, (3) cereals, grains, and nuts, and (4) eggs, milk, and cheese.
4. From old magazines, cut pictures to represent each of these categories.
5. Glue a magazine picture on each train car to represent one category.
6. Place all of the other pictures in the envelope.

HOW YOU PLAY

Remove the pictures from the envelope and sort them by placing each one in the appropriate train car.

VARIATION

Choose different categories. For example, you might use four animal groups, such as birds, fish, mammals, and reptiles.

Egg Carton Zoo

Make a zooful of animals from an empty egg carton or two.

WHAT YOU NEED

- [ ] at least one empty egg carton
- [ ] a pair of scissors
- [ ] some tape or glue
- [ ] tempera paint
- [ ] several paintbrushes
- [ ] scraps of construction paper
- [ ] assorted objects from your odds and ends collection

WHAT YOU DO

1. Cut the egg carton into individual cups and clusters of cups.
2. Make these cups look like animals by adding ears, legs, and wings cut from egg carton scraps and/or other materials.

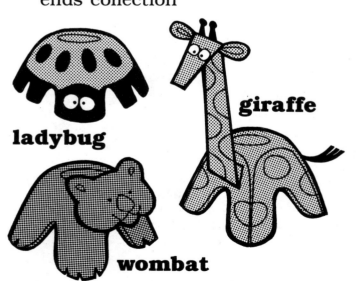

ladybug

giraffe

wombat

turtle

mouse

crab

Egg Carton Zoo
(continued)

3. Paint your animal. If you are using an egg carton made of polystyrene foam, add a small amount of laundry detergent to your paint to help it adhere to the slick surface of the carton.

4. Tape or glue on features cut from construction paper, yarn, cardboard, and/or fabric.

spider

chicken

cricket

armadillo

butterfly

rabbit

Egg Carton Big Mouths

Using your imagination and objects from your odds and ends collection, turn empty egg cartons and hinged food storage boxes into creatures with big personalities and big mouths to match!

WHAT YOU NEED

☐ empty egg cartons and/or hinged polystyrene foam food boxes
☐ a pair of scissors with sharp points
☐ some masking tape
☐ glue
☐ assorted objects from your odds and ends collection

WHAT YOU DO

1. Cut the egg carton into thirds.
2. Reinforce the hinge with masking tape.
3. Decide whether to turn the egg carton so that the humps are up or down. Turning them up might create a perfect place for frog eyes, while turning them down might make rabbit or squirrel cheeks.

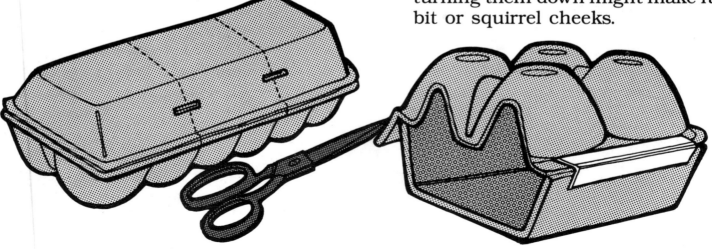

Egg Carton Big Mouths
(continued)

4. With the point of the closed scissors, poke and twist two finger holes in the side of the carton, above the hinge.

5. Using objects from your odds and ends collection, add eyes, nose, mouth, ears, teeth, horns, hair, and other creature features.

Egg Carton Creature

WHAT YOU NEED

- [ ] an empty egg carton
- [ ] assorted paper and plastic trash, including cardboard tubes, paper plates and cups, picnic knives and forks, napkins, and straws
- [ ] bits and pieces from your odds and ends collection
- [ ] a box lid, tablet back, or empty pizza box for the base
- [ ] a stapler and staples
- [ ] some tape and/or glue

WHAT YOU DO

1. Using tape, glue, and/or staples, assemble the listed materials to create a creature.
2. To make your creature more stable, mount it on a base.
3. Just for fun, name your creature and write a story about something it does, someone it meets, or an adventure it has.

BOTTLES
&
CANS

Tin Canimals

Create an amazing array of creatures using lots of recycled cans and a little imagination.

WHAT YOU NEED

- [ ] empty cans in various shapes and sizes
- [ ] a roll of adhesive or masking tape
- [ ] a tape measure and a ruler
- [ ] a pencil
- [ ] some construction, shelf, or butcher paper
- [ ] scraps of paper and fabric
- [ ] assorted objects from your odds and ends collection
- [ ] a pair of scissors
- [ ] some tape or glue
- [ ] a little imagination

WHAT YOU DO

1. Remove the paper labels or wrappers from the cans.
2. Wash and dry the cans thoroughly.
3. If the top edges of the cans are sharp or rough, carefully cover them with adhesive or masking tape so that you will not cut yourself when you handle the cans.
4. Using the tape measure, measure around the can. Write down this measurement.

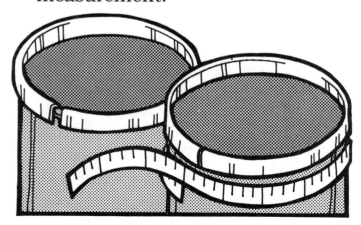

Tin Canimals
(continued)

5. Using either the tape measure or the ruler, measure the can from top to bottom. Write down this measurement.

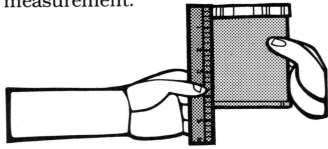

6. From the construction, shelf, or butcher paper, cut a rectangle that measures the same from top to bottom as the can and measures 1/2 inch more in length than the can measures around.

7. Wrap this paper rectangle around the can and tape or glue it where the ends overlap.

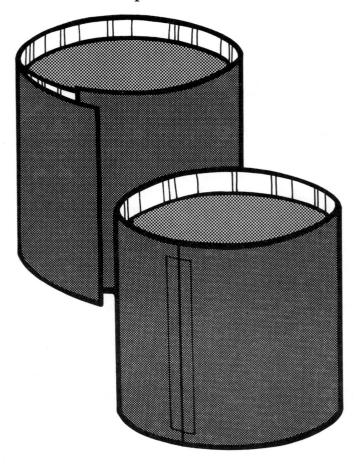

Tin Canimals
(continued)

8. Turn the covered can into a canimal by taping or gluing on such creature features as eyes, ears, a nose, a mouth, teeth, whiskers, horns, and a tail.

9. Use canimals to hold pencils, pens, crayons, or other art and desk supplies.

Tin Can Stilts

WHAT YOU NEED

- [ ] two large empty cans (juice or coffee)
- [ ] a punch-type can opener
- [ ] a roll of adhesive or masking tape
- [ ] 10 feet of lightweight rope
- [ ] a pair of scissors

WHAT YOU DO

1. Remove the paper labels or wrappers from the cans.
2. Rinse and dry the cans.
3. Turn both cans upside down so that the open ends are at the bottom.
4. With the can opener, punch two holes opposite each other in the sides at the closed end of each can.
5. Carefully cover the sharp edges of the holes with tape.
6. Cut the rope in half.
7. Loop one 5-foot length of rope through the holes in each can.
8. Adjust the length of the ropes so that you can easily reach them and hold them taut when you stand up straight on your stilts.

9. Knot the rope to hold it in place.
10. Walk on your tin can stilts. Listen to the hollow clonking sound they make as you stomp along the sidewalk. Notice the interesting tracks they leave in the dirt.

Walkie-Talkies

WHAT YOU NEED

- [ ] two empty tin cans with one end removed
- [ ] a roll of adhesive or masking tape
- [ ] a long nail
- [ ] a hammer
- [ ] about 3 feet of nylon fish line
- [ ] two medium-sized buttons
- [ ] a friend

WHAT YOU DO

1. Remove the paper labels or wrappers from the cans.
2. Rinse and dry the cans.
3. If the top edges of the cans are sharp or rough, carefully cover them with a small amount of adhesive or masking tape so that you will not cut yourself when you handle the cans.

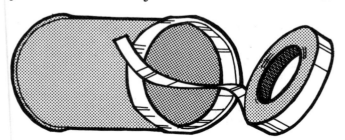

4. Make a hole in the center of the closed end of each can by hammering the nail part way into it.
5. Thread one end of the nylon fish line through the hole in one can and tie it to a button.

Walkie-Talkies
(continued)

6. Thread the other end of the nylon line through the other can and tie it to the other button.

7. Have your friend take one can and walk away until the line is tight.

8. While your friend talks into the open end of one can, hold the open end of the other can to your ear and listen.

Maracas

A **maraca** is a dried gourd or a rattle that is shaped like a gourd and contains dried seeds or pebbles. Maracas are used as percussion instruments, especially in Latin America.

WHAT YOU NEED

- [ ] two empty soda cans
- [ ] a roll of masking tape
- [ ] some seeds or unpopped popcorn
- [ ] a pair of scissors
- [ ] feathers, lace, ribbon, rick-rack, or other things from your odds and ends collection
- [ ] some glue

WHAT YOU DO

1. Rinse the cans and allow them to drain.
2. Carefully drop some seeds or unpopped popcorn into one can through the drinking hole in the top.
3. Cover the hole with masking tape to keep the seeds inside.
4. Decorate the can by attaching some fun or fancy things from your odds and ends collection to it. If your can has a pull tab, tie some ribbon through the loop.
5. Repeat steps 2 through 4 for the second can so that you will have a pair of maracas.

VARIATION

Put some pennies, pebbles, or paper clips in your cans instead of seeds.

Rockets Away

WHAT YOU NEED

- ☐ tin cans of assorted sizes
- ☐ a roll of adhesive, duct, or masking tape
- ☐ an old funnel
- ☐ some paint
- ☐ a paintbrush
- ☐ some flag, letter, or insignia stickers or decals

WHAT YOU DO

1. Stack the cans to simulate the shape of a rocket by placing the largest can on the bottom and using smaller cans as you build toward the top.
2. Tape or glue the cans together.
3. Use an old funnel or some other cone-shaped object for the nose of the rocket.
4. Paint your stacked cans to look like a rocket.
5. Add appropriate stickers or decals.

Tuna Toss

WHAT YOU NEED

- [ ] six empty tuna cans
- [ ] some masking tape
- [ ] a roll of duct tape (optional)
- [ ] a felt-tipped marking pen
- [ ] several small bean bags, six pennies, or some large buttons

WHAT YOU DO

1. Remove the paper label or wrapper from the cans.
2. Rinse and dry the cans.
3. If the top edges of the cans are sharp or rough, carefully cover them with duct or masking tape so that you will not cut yourself when you handle them.
4. With duct or masking tape, fasten the cans together to form a triangle as shown.
5. To number the cans, place a piece of masking tape on the bottom of each can, and write a number on each piece of tape.
6. Standing behind a line or a specified distance from your tuna can target, toss the bean bags, pennies, or buttons into the cans.
7. Total the numbers from six separate tosses to determine your score.
8. Challenge a friend to a game or two of Tuna Toss.

Egg-citing Mosaic Can

WHAT YOU NEED

- [ ] an empty vegetable, soup, or coffee can
- [ ] the shells from several eggs
- [ ] paper towels
- [ ] a sheet of waxed paper
- [ ] a rolling pin
- [ ] two paintbrushes
- [ ] some glue
- [ ] some paint
- [ ] a piece of aluminum foil (optional)

WHAT YOU DO

1. Remove the paper label or wrapper from the can.
2. Rinse and dry the can.
3. Rinse the eggshells and lay them on paper towels. Place a layer of paper towels over the eggshells and pat the shells dry.
4. Place the dry eggshells on a sheet of waxed paper.
5. Use the rolling pin to crush and spread the shells.
6. Brush glue over the outside of the can.
7. While the glue is wet, roll the can in the crushed eggshells.
8. Stand the can on a piece of foil or on the sheet of waxed paper and allow the glue to dry thoroughly.
9. Paint the can. Shiny or metallic paint will create an especially interesting look.
10. Use the decorated can to hold hard candies, pens, pencils, crayons, paintbrushes, or other desk or craft supplies.

Tin Can Totem Pole

A **totem** is an animal or plant that serves as a symbol for a family, clan, or tribe. A **totem pole** is a pillar carved and painted with a series of these symbols. For some people, totem poles are records of family history or of ancestral accomplishments.

WHAT YOU NEED

- [ ] five or more tin cans of the same circumference
- [ ] some glue
- [ ] some masking tape
- [ ] papier-mâché mixture (see page 14)
- [ ] pieces of cardboard or tag board
- [ ] a pair of sharp scissors
- [ ] paint in a variety of bright colors
- [ ] several paintbrushes

WHAT YOU DO

1. Stack the cans.
2. Apply glue to the can rims where the stacked cans touch.
3. Once the glue has dried, reinforce the glued seams with masking tape.
4. From cardboard or tag board, cut wings, noses, feet, beaks, and other animal features.

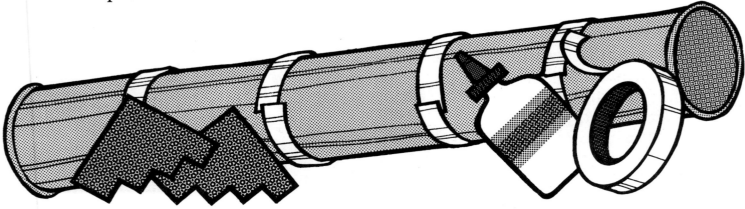

Tin Can Totem Pole
(continued)

5. Tape these features in place on the pole.
6. One at a time, dip the newspaper strips in the papier-mâché mixture and place them on the pole.
7. Cover the entire pole with a single layer of dampened strips.
8. Allow the strips to dry thoroughly.
9. Apply two additional layers of strips, allowing time for one layer to dry before adding the next.
10. When your totem pole is dry, paint it and add some special symbols and original designs.

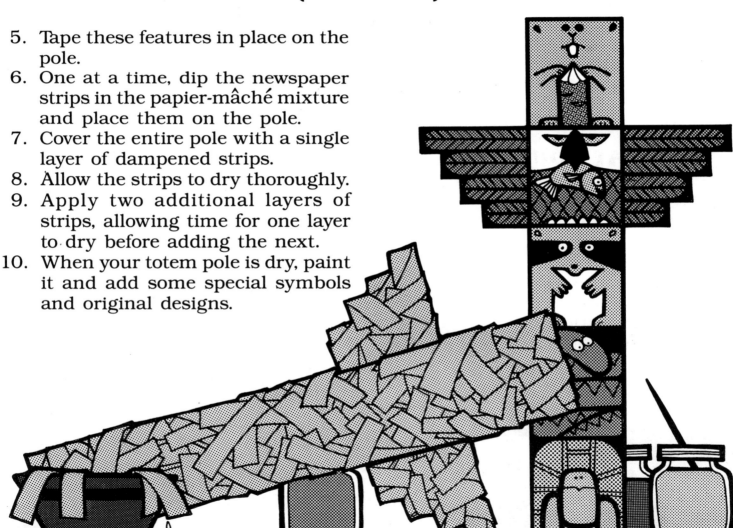

Tin Can Lantern

Tin can lanterns were popular in Colonial America. Before household electricity was common, these lanterns were used to shield lighted candles from the wind as they were carried from room to room. Make your own tin can lantern for light or for decoration.

WHAT YOU NEED

- [ ] a coffee can with the lid removed
- [ ] a permanent marking pen
- [ ] a soft, absorbent terry cloth towel
- [ ] nails of different sizes
- [ ] a hammer
- [ ] a wire coat hanger
- [ ] wire cutters
- [ ] a pair of pliers
- [ ] one household candle about an inch *shorter* than the coffee can
- [ ] some matches

WHAT YOU DO

1. Create a design on the coffee can by making dots with the marking pen.
2. Fill the can with water.
3. Put the can in a freezer and leave it for about 24 hours, until the water in the can has frozen into a solid block of ice.

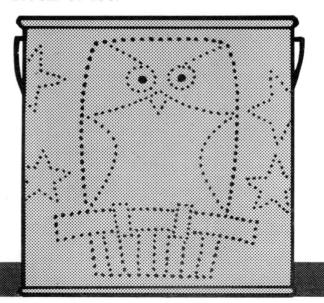

Tin Can Lantern
(continued)

4. Take the can out of the freezer and lay it on a soft, absorbent terry cloth towel.

5. Carefully turn each dot of your design into a hole by hammering a nail into it. To vary the sizes of the holes, use nails of different diameters.

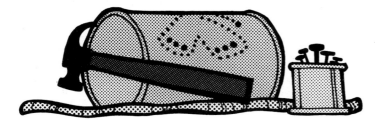

6. Punch a fairly large hole on each side of the can near the top.

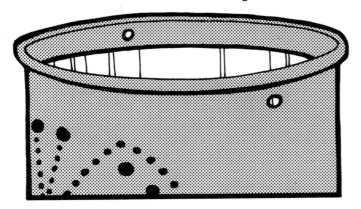

7. Cut a 10- to 12-inch section out of the straight crossing piece of the coat hanger.

8. To make a handle for your tin can lantern, loop the ends of the coat hanger through the large holes in the sides of the can.

9. Using the pliers, bend the hanger ends up.

Tin Can Lantern
(continued)

10. When all of the holes have been made, turn the can upside down and allow the melting ice to slide out.

11. Leave the can upside down for a while so that the inside will drain and dry. In step 12, the wax will not adhere to the bottom of the can if the surface is still wet.

12. Light the candle. Hold the lighted candle so that the melting wax will drop on the bottom of the can.

13. While the wax on the bottom of the can is warm and soft, stand the candle upright in it.

CAUTION

When the candle in your lantern is burning, do not place it near curtains or other highly flammable fabric. And never leave a burning candle unattended. Always blow out the candle before you leave the room.

Tin Can Lantern Pattern

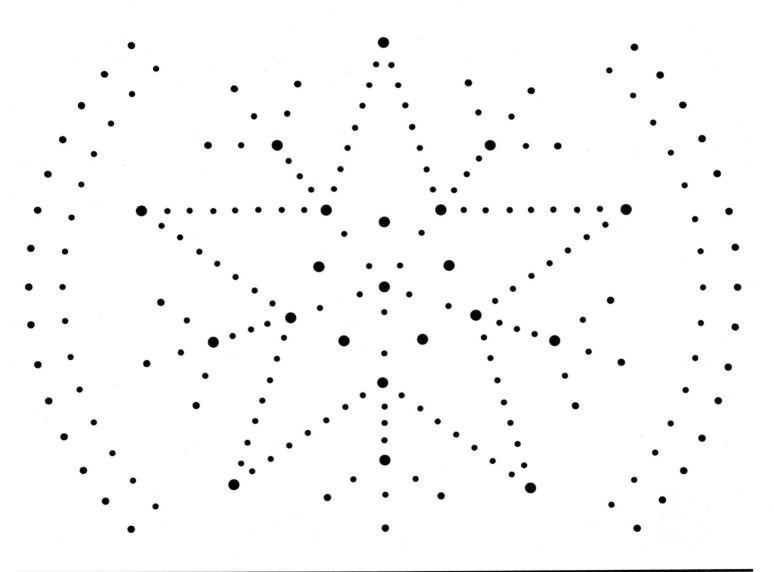

Decorate a Bottle

WHAT YOU NEED

- [ ] an empty bottle or jar
- [ ] tissue paper in assorted colors
- [ ] a pair of scissors
- [ ] some liquid starch
- [ ] a shallow, wide-mouthed container (for example, a baby food jar or a margarine tub)
- [ ] a paintbrush

WHAT YOU DO

1. Remove the paper wrapper or label from the bottle or jar.
2. Rinse the bottle or jar and allow it to dry.
3. Cut or tear the tissue paper into small pieces.
4. Pour the starch into the container.

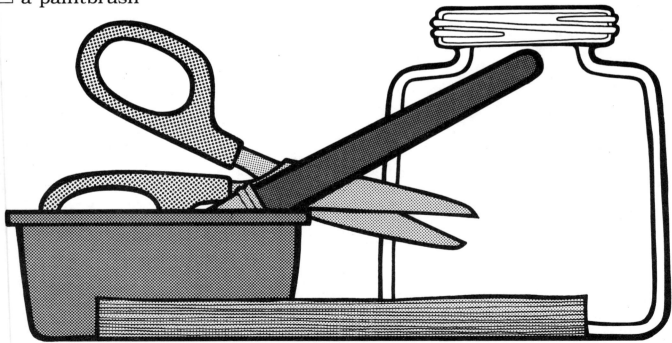

Decorate a Bottle
(continued)

5. With one hand, hold a piece of tissue paper on the bottle. With the other hand, brush liquid starch over the tissue paper, onto the bottle. The starch will make the tissue paper stick to the bottle.

6. Repeat step 5, overlapping the pieces of tissue paper, until the bottle is completely covered.
7. Allow the starch to dry.
8. Use the bottles and jars you decorate in this way as pencil holders, vases, and desk organizers.

Salt Surprises

WHAT YOU NEED

- [ ] an empty bottle or jar with a lid
- [ ] a box of salt
- [ ] chalk in several different colors
- [ ] several sheets of notebook paper
- [ ] a cup for each color of chalk

WHAT YOU DO

1. Remove the paper wrapper or label from the bottle or jar.
2. Rinse the bottle or jar and allow it to dry.
3. Pour some of the salt on one sheet of notebook paper.
4. Rub chalk over the salt until the salt is the same color as the chalk.
5. Lift the sheet of paper carefully by the edges, and pour the colored salt into a cup.
6. Repeat steps 3 through 5 for every color of chalk, using a different sheet of paper and a different cup each time.
7. Pour one color of salt into your bottle or jar.
8. Repeat with a second color, varying the shape and thickness of the layers.
9. Continue layering the salt to the top of the bottle or jar. Do not shake the bottle or jar, or mix the layers.
10. Cover the bottle or jar tightly and let it stand overnight.
11. When the salt has settled, add more salt and cover tightly again.
12. Enjoy the view!

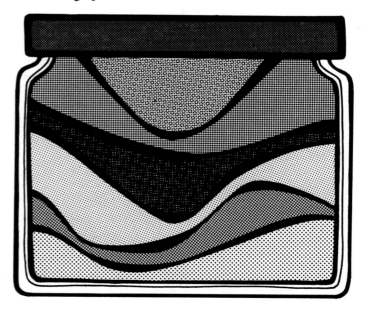

Make a Montage

WHAT YOU NEED

☐ an empty glass bottle
☐ colorful pictures cut from magazines
☐ a pair of scissors
☐ some white glue thinned with water
☐ a paintbrush

WHAT YOU DO

1. Cut the pictures into geometric shapes of different sizes.
2. Brush glue on a small area of the bottle.
3. Press the geometric shapes on the wet glue, one at a time, overlapping the edges.
4. Repeat steps 2 and 3 until the bottle is completely covered.
5. Allow the glue to dry.
6. Finish by brushing a coat of thinned glue over the entire bottle.
7. Allow this coat of glue to dry before using the bottle to hold something fascinating or fun.

VARIATION

Decorate your bottle to reflect a specific hobby or theme that interests you, such as cars or sports.

Bottle Sculptures

WHAT YOU NEED

- [ ] a plastic detergent bottle with the cap or lid removed
- [ ] 2 cups of salt or sand
- [ ] papier-mâché mixture (see page 14)
- [ ] old newspapers
- [ ] some masking tape
- [ ] a pair of scissors
- [ ] paintbrushes
- [ ] tempera paint in several colors
- [ ] yarn, buttons, and other things from your odds and ends collection
- [ ] some glue

WHAT YOU DO

1. Pour the salt or sand into the bottle to keep it from tipping over while you work.
2. Tear one sheet of newspaper in half.
3. Wad one half into a tight ball.
4. Place this ball in the center of the other half.
5. Grasp the four corners and twist them to hold the ball in place.
6. Insert the twisted end of the newspaper into the top of your plastic bottle so that only the ball shows.

Bottle Sculptures
(continued)

7. Tape the ball in place.
8. Cut some of the remaining sheets of newspaper into strips.
9. One at a time, dip the newspaper strips into the papier-mâché mixture and lay them over the ball and bottle.
10. Cover the entire ball and bottle with a single layer of dampened strips.
11. Allow the strips to dry thoroughly.
12. Repeat steps 9 through 11 three times. As you do so, shape arms and a skirt or legs.
13. Paint a face, body, clothes, arms, legs, feet, and other features on your bottle sculpture.
14. Add other details. You may want to glue on yarn for hair, buttons for eyes, and lace, rick-rack, or other decorations.

Soda Bottle Greenhouse

WHAT YOU NEED

- [ ] a large clear plastic soda bottle
- [ ] a coping saw or other small handsaw
- [ ] an X-acto knife
- [ ] some potting soil
- [ ] a package of seeds
- [ ] some water

WHAT YOU DO

1. Using the saw, carefully cut off the top third of the bottle and save it.
2. Put soil in the remaining two-thirds of the bottle.
3. Plant the seeds according to the directions on the package.
4. Sprinkle enough water on the soil to make it damp but not so much that it becomes muddy.
5. Using either the saw or the knife, cut 2-inch slits in the top portion of the bottle as shown.
6. Put the top portion of the bottle over the bottom portion.
7. Place your soda bottle greenhouse in a warm, well-lighted place.
8. Sprinkle lightly with water if needed, but do not overwater.
9. Watch your greenhouse garden grow!

Bleach Bottle Beach Toys

WHAT YOU NEED

- ☐ one clean, plastic bleach bottle
- ☐ a pocket or paring knife
- ☐ a pair of sharp scissors
- ☐ a 12- to 16-inch length of cord or laundry line

WHAT YOU DO

1. Using the knife, make a slit in the side of the bleach bottle about halfway between the top and bottom.
2. Insert a scissor point in this slit and carefully cut the bottle in half.
3. Use the top half of the bleach bottle as a sand scoop or funnel.
4. Use the bottom half as a beach bucket.
5. To add a handle, use the knife to make two slits about 1-1/2 inches below the top of the bucket on opposite sides.
6. Enlarge these holes with the scissors.
7. Insert one end of the cord through the hole on one side of the bucket and knot it.
8. Insert the other end of the cord through the hole on the other side of the bucket and knot it.

Candleholder

This candleholder is ideal for use as a table decoration at picnics, patio parties, and barbecues.

WHAT YOU NEED

- [ ] one empty half-gallon bleach bottle
- [ ] a pocket or paring knife
- [ ] a pair of sharp scissors
- [ ] rick-rack and other things from your odds and ends collection
- [ ] some felt pieces or fabric scraps
- [ ] white glue
- [ ] a candle whose diameter is similar to that of the bottle spout
- [ ] some aluminum foil

WHAT YOU DO

1. Rinse the bleach bottle and allow it to drain and dry thoroughly.
2. Using the knife, make a slit in the side of the bleach bottle about two-thirds of the way up from the bottom.
3. Insert one scissor point in the slit and carefully cut the bottle into two pieces.
4. To turn the top portion of the bottle into a decorative candleholder, glue rick-rack around the spout, base, and handle.
5. Add fun or fancy shapes cut from felt pieces or fabric scraps.
6. If the base of the candle is too large for the bottle spout, use the knife to carve away a small amount of the wax.
7. If the base of the candle is too small for the bottle spout, wrap the base with a strip of aluminum foil and place the candle in the spout, wrinkling and crushing the foil as needed for a safe, snug fit.

Create a Can Cover

Use an empty plastic bottle to conceal a cleanser can or other unsightly container in the kitchen, in the bathroom, or elsewhere.

WHAT YOU NEED

- [ ] one empty plastic bottle large enough to cover the can you wish to hide
- [ ] a ruler at least 12 inches long
- [ ] a pencil and/or a permanent marker
- [ ] a pocket or paring knife
- [ ] a pair of sharp scissors
- [ ] some fabric or felt scraps
- [ ] assorted objects from your odds and ends collection
- [ ] white glue

WHAT YOU DO

1. Rinse the plastic bottle and allow it to drain and dry thoroughly.
2. With the ruler, measure the height of the container you wish to conceal and write down this measurement.
3. Holding the ruler next to the plastic bottle, measure up the side of the bottle and place a mark 1/2 inch *higher* than the height of the container you plan to hide.
4. Using the knife, cut a slit in the side of the plastic bottle where you placed the mark.
5. Insert a scissor point in this slit and carefully cut off the top of the bottle.
6. Turn the bottle upside down so that the bottom becomes the top.
7. Decorate the bottle with shapes cut from fabric or felt scraps and with ribbon, rick-rack, or other things from your odds and ends collection.
8. Use your beautifully decorated bottle to hide an ugly can.

Decorate a Dog

WHAT YOU NEED

- [ ] a large empty plastic bleach bottle
- [ ] a pocket or paring knife
- [ ] a pair of sharp scissors
- [ ] pieces of felt in such colors as black, brown, pink, and/or red
- [ ] four plastic bottle caps or corks for feet
- [ ] some wire (optional)
- [ ] buttons, bells, bows, and yarn from your odds and ends collection
- [ ] glue

WHAT YOU DO

1. Rinse the bleach bottle and allow it to drain and dry thoroughly.
2. To make a nose, cover the bleach bottle cap with black felt.
3. Cut a tongue from red or pink felt.
4. Cut ears from brown or black felt.
5. Glue the tongue in place under the nose.
6. Cut a slit in either side of the head, insert an ear in each slit, and glue it in place.
7. Glue on the bottle caps or corks for feet.
8. To make a simple tail, braid some yarn and glue it on.
9. To make a stand-up tail, shape a piece of wire to curve over your dog's back. Glue brown or black felt to the wire. Cut a slit at the end of the dog, insert the tail wire, and glue the tail in place.
10. Decorate your pooch by gluing on buttons, bells, and/or bows from your odds and ends collection.

Decorate a Dinosaur

WHAT YOU NEED

- ☐ two large empty plastic bleach bottles or one bottle and some construction paper
- ☐ a pocket or paring knife
- ☐ a pair of sharp scissors
- ☐ four plastic bottle caps or corks for feet
- ☐ pieces of felt in such colors as black, brown, green, pink, and/or red for features
- ☐ other things from your odds and ends collection
- ☐ masking tape and glue

WHAT YOU DO

1. Rinse the bleach bottles and allow them to drain and dry thoroughly.
2. Fashion appropriate facial features from felt and glue them to one bottle.
3. Glue bottle caps or corks to this same bottle for feet.
4. Decorate your dinosaur by gluing on spots, scales, bony plates, or other pieces and parts using the other bottle, the construction paper, and/or things from your odds and ends collection.

Flower Basket Bonanza

Turn an empty plastic bleach bottle into a flower basket.

WHAT YOU NEED

☐ an empty plastic bleach bottle
☐ a pocket or paring knife
☐ a pair of sharp scissors
☐ a ruler
☐ a pencil
☐ two brads or some glue

WHAT YOU DO

1. Rinse the bottle and allow it to drain and dry thoroughly.
2. Using the knife, make a slit in the side of the bottle, about 6 inches up from the bottom. Save the top part of the bottle for use later in making a handle for your basket.

3. Insert one scissor point in the slit and carefully cut the bottle into two pieces.

4. Cut vertical slits 3/4 inches apart, leaving a one-inch margin at the bottom as shown.

Flower Basket Bonanza
(continued)

5. Wrap each strip around the pencil and curl it down.

6. To make a handle for your basket, cut a strip one inch wide and 18 to 20 inches long from the top part of the bottle, which you saved.

7. Glue the handle to the inside of your basket or attach it with brads.
8. To fill your empty basket with an egg cup bouquet, see page 51.

Piggy Bank

WHAT YOU NEED

- [ ] a plastic bleach or milk bottle, a water jug, or some other similar plastic container
- [ ] four corks, bottle caps, or empty thread spools
- [ ] white glue
- [ ] a pocket or paring knife
- [ ] a pair of sharp scissors
- [ ] tissue paper in a variety of colors
- [ ] acrylic polymer medium
- [ ] paintbrushes
- [ ] a pencil
- [ ] scraps of pink, brown, black, and white felt
- [ ] a pink or brown pipe cleaner for the tail

WHAT YOU DO

1. Remove the bottle cap and set it aside for safe keeping.
2. Rinse the bottle and allow it to drain and dry thoroughly.
3. To add legs, turn the bottle on its side with the handle up. Glue the corks, bottle caps, or spools to what is now the pig's stomach.
4. Let the glue dry thoroughly.
5. With the knife and/or scissors, carefully cut a slit about 1-1/2 inches long in the pig's back to serve as a coin slot.

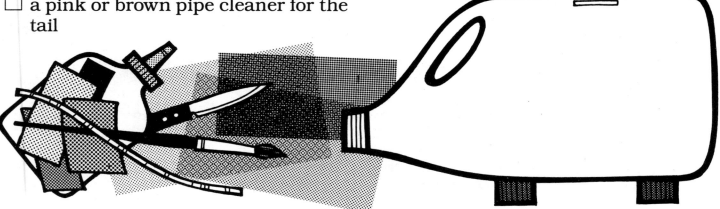

Piggy Bank
(continued)

6. Cut the tissue paper into 2-inch squares, or into circles or triangles of similar size.
7. With a brush, paint a small area of the bottle with medium.
8. Place the cut tissue shapes over the medium on the container, allowing them to overlap. Do not put tissue paper or medium over the coin slit or over the grooves for screwing on the cap.

9. Paint medium over the tissue shapes, smoothing them flat.
10. Repeat steps 7, 8, and 9 until the pig's body and legs are completely covered with tissue.

Piggy Bank
(continued)

11. To make the nose, place the cap on a piece of pink felt and trace around it once.
12. To make the eyes, place the cap on a piece of white felt and trace around it twice.
13. Cut out the resulting pink and white felt circles.
14. Glue the nose circle to the end of the cap.
15. Glue the eye circles to the container near the handle, on either side of the snout, as shown.

16. If you wish, cut out and add smaller black or white felt circles to the nose for nostrils and to the eyes for pupils. Similarly, add brown or black felt eyelashes and eyebrows.
17. To form the tail, curl the pipe cleaner around a pencil.
18. Glue the curled pipe cleaner to the end of the pig or cut a small slit in the end of the pig, insert the end of the pipe cleaner, and glue it in place.

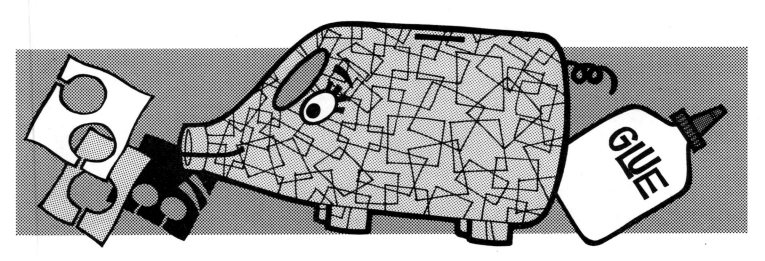

BAGS, CUPS, TUBES & MORE

Op-Art Beads

WHAT YOU NEED

- [ ] a piece of cardboard or tag board that is at least 5 inches wide and 2 inches high
- [ ] a pencil and a ruler
- [ ] a pair of scissors
- [ ] brightly colored pages torn from old magazines
- [ ] twelve toothpicks or skewers
- [ ] white glue
- [ ] a needle with a large eye
- [ ] some yarn, a leather thong, or a spool of heavy thread

WHAT YOU DO

1. Using the pencil and ruler, draw a tall, narrow triangle that is 4 inches wide and 1-1/2 inches high on a piece of cardboard or tagboard.
2. Cut out this triangle carefully so that the sides are straight and it can be used as a pattern.
3. Using this pattern, cut at least twelve triangles from the magazine pages.

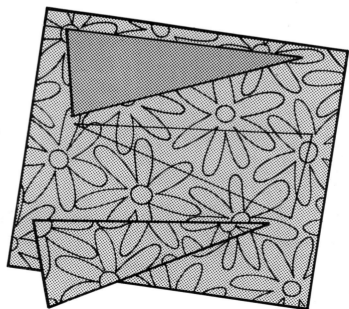

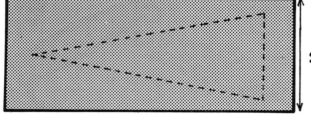

5 inches

2 inches

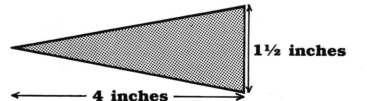

1½ inches

4 inches

Op-Art Beads
(continued)

4. Wrap the base of one triangle around a toothpick or skewer and roll it tightly.
5. Glue down the pointed end of the roll to hold it in place.
6. Repeat steps 4 and 5 until you have made about a dozen beads.
7. Allow the glue to dry.
8. Gently slide the beads off the toothpicks or skewers.
9. Using the needle, string the beads on a piece of yarn, a leather thong, or heavy thread.
10. Knot both ends of the yarn, leather, or thread so that the beads will not slide off.

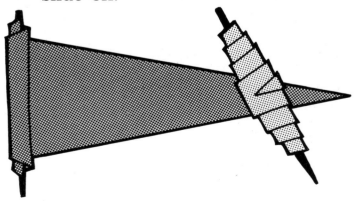

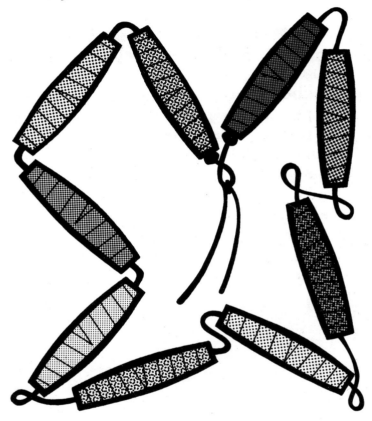

VARIATION
Before stringing the beads, paint them with acrylic polymer medium or with dilute white glue to harden the surface and make them shine.

Paper Curls

WHAT YOU NEED

- [ ] brightly colored pages torn from old magazines
- [ ] a pair of scissors
- [ ] some white glue
- [ ] the lid from a margarine tub or bottle
- [ ] a pencil
- [ ] one sheet of construction paper

WHAT YOU DO

1. Cut the magazine pages into strips that are 1/4 inch wide and 8 inches long.
2. Pour a small amount of glue into the lid.
3. Wrap one strip tightly around the pencil.
4. Carefully slide the curled strip off the pencil.

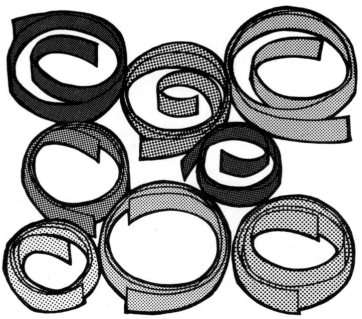

Paper Curls
(continued)

5. Dip one edge of the curled strip into the glue.
6. Place the curled strip on the sheet of construction paper so that the glue side is down.
7. Repeat steps 3, 4, 5, and 6 to form a design of curls on the sheet of paper.

8. Allow the paper to lie flat while the glue dries.
9. Hang your paper curl design where it can be seen and enjoyed.

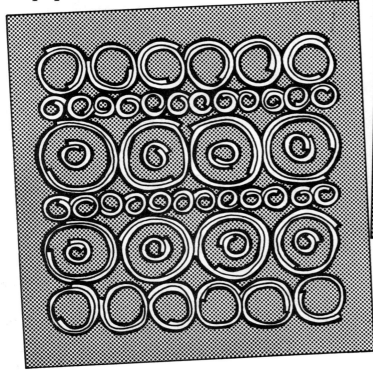

VARIATION
Draw a picture on art or construction paper. Use curled strips of paper to add color and texture to your picture.

Cardboard-and-Scrap Collage

A **collage** is a picture or design made by gluing various materials on a surface.

WHAT YOU NEED

- [ ] an assortment of things from your odds and ends collection
- [ ] a piece of corrugated cardboard measuring about 9 inches by 12 inches
- [ ] a pencil
- [ ] a pair of sharp scissors
- [ ] some white glue
- [ ] a piece of string or yarn about 18 inches long
- [ ] a stapler and staples

WHAT YOU DO

1. Review your odds and ends collection for interesting objects you might use to make your collage. For example, you might consider bottle caps, braid, burlap, buttons, corks, cotton balls, fabric scraps, felt, feathers, lace, rickrack, and/or yarn.

Cardboard-and-Scrap Collage
(continued)

2. With the pencil, draw scallops, square corners, zigzags, or some other interesting pattern along the top and bottom of the cardboard.

3. Using a pair of sharp scissors, carefully cut along the pencil lines you have drawn.

4. For added interest, cut several holes in the cardboard.

Cardboard-and-Scrap Collage
(continued)

5. Arrange the objects you have selected on the cardboard so that they make an interesting picture or design.

6. When you are satisfied with your design, glue each object in place.

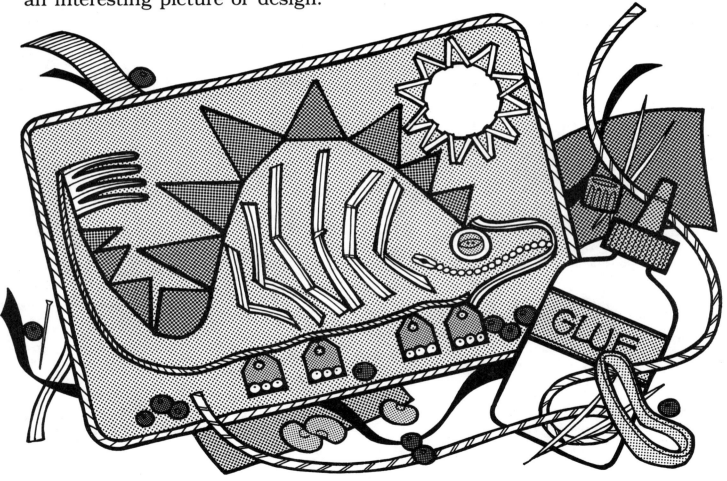

Cardboard-and-Scrap Collage
(continued)

7. Staple a piece of string or yarn to the back of the cardboard at the top right and left corners.
8. Hang your collage where others can see and enjoy it.

VARIATION

Make a collage of found natural objects instead of things from your odds and ends collection. For example, you might use leaves, flowers, feathers, bits of wood or bark, and shells. But be careful that the objects you use are things nature no longer needs.

Paper Dot Mosaic

A **mosaic** is a surface decoration that is created by arranging small pieces of variously colored material so that they form patterns or pictures. This project is lots of fun, but it takes a long time. Spread the fun over several sessions or invite some friends to help.

WHAT YOU NEED

- [ ] some old magazines and/or scraps of construction or other colored paper
- [ ] a one-hole punch
- [ ] several empty margarine tubs or other similar shallow, widemouthed containers with lids
- [ ] a piece of white poster board measuring about 9 inches by 12 inches
- [ ] a pencil
- [ ] some white glue
- [ ] a measuring cup
- [ ] a paintbrush
- [ ] some toothpicks or straight pins

WHAT YOU DO

1. Punch lots of paper dots from the pages of old magazines and/or from scraps of construction or other colored paper.
2. Separate the dots according to color, storing dots of each color in a different margarine tub.
3. Draw a simple outline shape on the poster board. For ideas, look at the shapes pictured on page 103.
4. Pour 1/4 cup of white glue into a margarine tub, add an equal amount of water, and stir until blended.
5. Brush thinned glue over a small area of the shape you outlined.

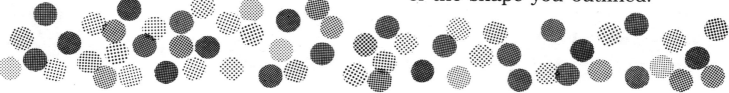

Paper Dot Mosaic
(continued)

6. Using a toothpick or straight pin, pick up the dots one at a time and place them on the glue, leaving tiny spaces between the dots.
7. Repeat steps 5 and 6 until your entire design is filled with colored dots.
8. Allow the poster board to lie flat while the glue dries.
9. Display your paper dot mosaic where it can be seen and enjoyed.

Rabbit Family Fun

Rabbits usually make their homes in burrows, but they sometimes hide in hollow logs. Make a rabbit family and write a poem or story about how they found this log and why they are hiding in it.

WHAT YOU NEED

- [ ] four cotton balls
- [ ] two tongue depressors or ice cream sticks
- [ ] a cardboard tube
- [ ] small pieces of stiff paper and/or tag board to make eyes and ears for the baby rabbits and a body for the mother rabbit
- [ ] a piece of string or thick thread for whiskers
- [ ] a pair of scissors
- [ ] some glue

WHAT YOU DO

1. Glue three of the cotton balls to one of the ice cream sticks.
2. Cut eyes and ears from the paper or tag board and glue these features to the three cotton balls.

Rabbit Family Fun
(continued)

3. Cut a mother rabbit from the stiff paper or tag board.
4. Glue her to one end of the other ice cream stick.
5. To make whiskers, cut two pieces of thread or string about 2-1/2 inches long and knot them together in the middle.
6. Glue thread or string whiskers and a cotton-ball tail to the mother rabbit.

7. Carefully cut one hole in the top and one hole in the bottom of the cardboard tube as shown.
8. Put the bottom of the mother rabbit's stick through these two holes so that she sits atop the log.
9. Slide the stick with the baby rabbits glued to it into one end of their hollow-log hiding place.

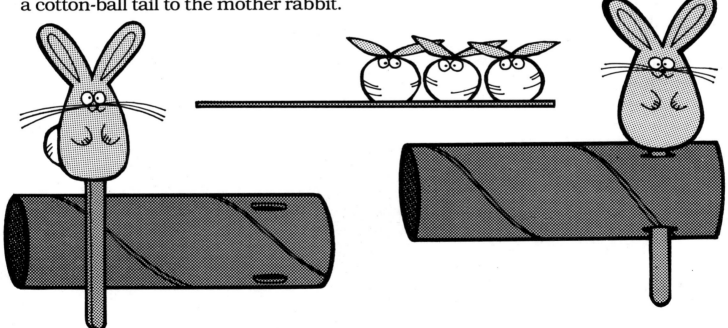

Kachina Dolls

Among the Hopi and other Pueblo Indians, a **kachina** is an ancestral spirit. The Indians believe that these spirits visit their villages from time to time to bring such gifts as strength and courage or adequate rain and abundant harvest.

From cottonwood root, the Indians fashion special dolls to represent these spirits. Indian children hang the dolls from the rafters of their houses to remind them of their spiritual heritage.

You can turn empty cardboard tubes into **kachina dolls** with some paint, some feathers, and your own creative touch.

WHAT YOU NEED

- several cardboard tubes
- a pair of sharp scissors
- a ruler and a pencil
- tempera paint in assorted colors, such as red, orange, yellow, green, blue, brown, black, peach, and turquoise
- several paintbrushes
- some felt-tipped marking pens
- white glue
- construction paper, beads, braid, fabric, felt, feathers, rick-rack, yarn, and other things from your odds and ends collection

Kachina Dolls
(continued)

WHAT YOU DO

1. Decide what your kachina doll will represent. Will it be a kind spirit or an angry one? What gift will it be able to bring?
2. Select one of the cardboard tubes.
3. If the tube you have selected is more than 6 to 8 inches long, you may wish to shorten it. Decide how tall you want your doll to be. Using the ruler, measure the tube and put a mark at the height you have chosen.
4. Holding the pencil in this spot and against the side of the tube, carefully turn the tube so that you draw a line around it.
5. Insert the sharp point of one scissor into the pencil mark and cut around the tube, following the pencil line and being careful *not* to bend or crush the tube.
6. Use paint to create shapes and patterns on your tube.
7. With paint, pens, and/or paper, add eyes, a nose, mouth, teeth, and other features.

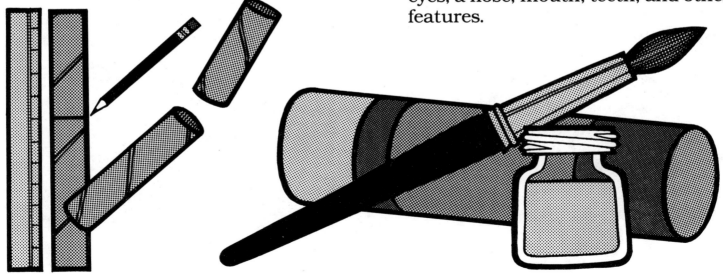

Kachina Dolls
(continued)

8. Decorate your dolls with fabric, felt, feathers, braid, yarn, and other things from your odds and ends collection.
9. Give your doll a name and create a special story, or legend, to go with it.

VARIATION

To add arms to your doll, carefully cut the narrow cardboard tubes from pants hangers into shorter segments, paint these tubes, and attach them to your doll using sturdy straight pins, paper clips, staples, or brads.

Roller Raceway

Create a series of chutes from cardboard tubes, connect them with joints made from other cardboard tubes, and watch a marble make its way down your meandering raceway.

Roller Raceway
(continued)

WHAT YOU NEED

☐ cardboard tubes of similar diameters but different lengths, for example, tubes from paper towel and waxed paper rolls and tubes from toilet paper rolls
☐ a pencil
☐ a ruler
☐ a pair of sharp scissors
☐ a coping saw
☐ some white glue
☐ a roll of masking tape
☐ several marbles

WHAT YOU DO

1. Plan your raceway. Think about how you will shape it. Consider how long and how steep it will be. Decide where you will put the corners and where you will put the straightaways. Use long tubes like the ones from paper towel or waxed paper rolls for straight chutes and short tubes like the ones from toilet paper rolls to create the corners and connect the chutes. Determine how many tubes you will need and where you will connect them.

2. Measure and mark the tubes to match your plans.

3. To make long open chutes, carefully cut some of your long cardboard tubes in half lengthwise using the scissors or the saw.

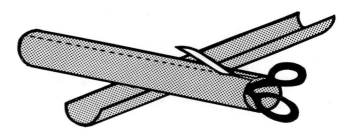

4. Use shorter tubes to connect these chutes. After inserting a chute end in the short tube, fasten it in place with masking tape or glue.

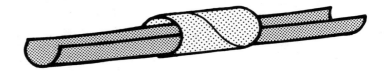

Roller Raceway
(continued)

5. Use shorter tubes to create corner joints also. Cut out a section as shown, bend the tube to close the opening created by your cut, and tape the tube to hold it in this bent position.

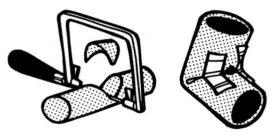

6. Arrange your raceway so that it slants downward. Use tables, chairs, books, and other objects to provide support.

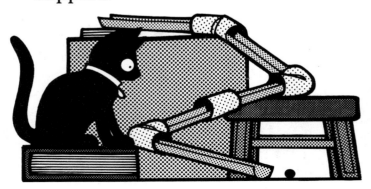

7. Roll a marble down your raceway. Time it to see how fast it goes. Challenge a friend to see whose marble can go down the raceway in the least amount of time or whose marble will go the farthest across the floor after exiting the raceway.

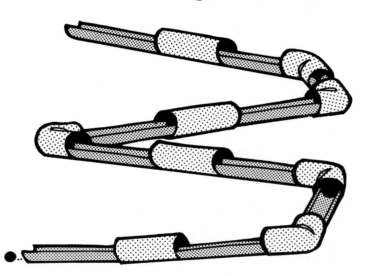

VARIATION
Use strips and scraps of self-adhesive paper to add pattern and color to your roller raceway.

Tube Sculptures

WHAT YOU NEED

- ☐ at least six to eight empty cardboard tubes from toilet paper, paper towel, or wrapping paper rolls
- ☐ some colored and/or patterned paper, for example, construction paper, shelf paper, or gift wrap
- ☐ self-adhesive dots, spots, strips, and labels
- ☐ decorative stickers and decals
- ☐ a pair of sharp scissors
- ☐ masking tape
- ☐ some white glue
- ☐ one piece of stiff or corrugated cardboard

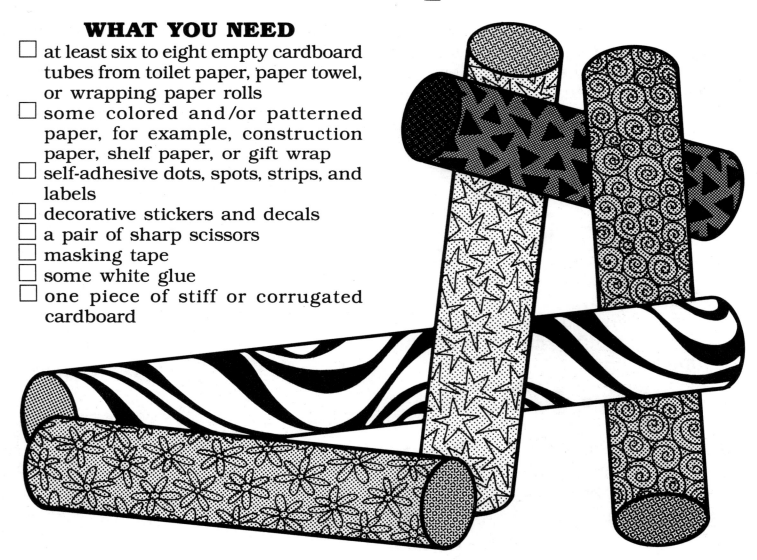

Tube Sculptures
(continued)

WHAT YOU DO

1. Use the tubes as they are or cut them to make them shorter and to create tubes of different lengths.
2. Wrap the tubes with colored or patterned paper (see page 13).
3. Add colored dots, spots, shapes, strips, or stickers.
4. Tape or glue the tubes together to create a sculpture.
5. To make a base for your sculpture, cover a piece of stiff or corrugated cardboard with colored or patterned paper.
6. Stand your sculpture on this base.

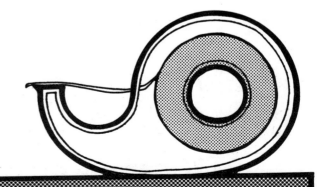

Desk Organizer

WHAT YOU NEED

- [ ] art or craft objects or stationery supplies to be organized
- [ ] a pencil, a ruler, and a piece of paper
- [ ] four to six empty cardboard tubes from toilet paper, paper towel, or wrapping paper rolls
- [ ] a pair of sharp scissors
- [ ] a coping saw
- [ ] some colored and/or patterned paper, for example, construction paper, shelf paper, or gift wrap
- [ ] felt or fabric scraps
- [ ] self-adhesive dots, spots, shapes, strips, and labels
- [ ] decorative stickers and decals
- [ ] some white glue
- [ ] a piece of stiff or corrugated cardboard for the base

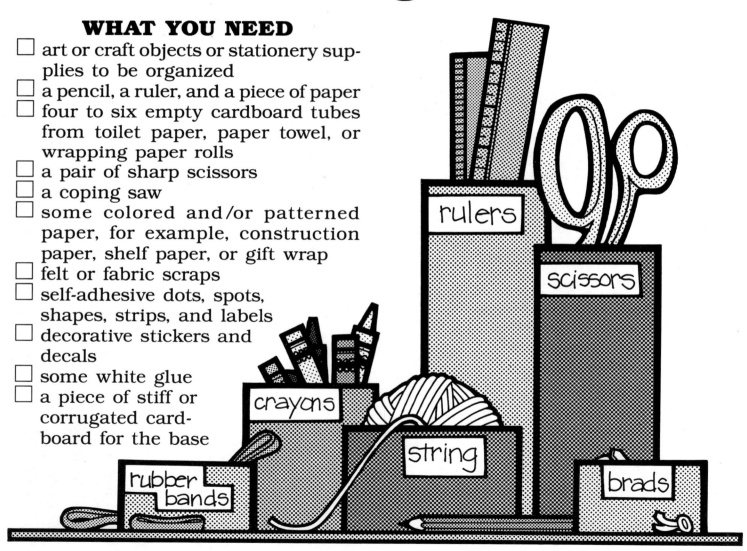

Desk Organizer
(continued)

WHAT YOU DO

1. Decide what kinds of art, craft, or stationery supplies you wish to organize. Consider crayons, paintbrushes, pens of various types or colors, pencils, brads, buttons, and paper clips.
2. Using the ruler, measure the lengths of the long, thin objects and write down these measurements.
3. Measure the lengths of the tubes carefully.
4. Based on these measurements, either select tubes that are about one-half to two-thirds the lengths of the objects you are organizing or use the coping saw to trim the tubes to the lengths you need.
5. Select one tube that is a bit wider in diameter than the others.
6. Cut this tube into several pieces about one inch long.
7. Wrap the tubes with colored or patterned paper (see page 13).
8. Add colored dots, spots, shapes, strips, or stickers.
9. Arrange the tubes in an interesting way.
10. Keeping the bases even, glue the sides of the tubes together.
11. If you wish, label the fronts of the tubes with letters cut from felt or fabric scraps or from self-adhesive paper.
12. Apply glue to the bottoms of the tubes and stand them on the base.
13. Allow the glue to dry thoroughly before beginning to use your desk organizer.

cut

wrap

arrange

label

Cup Puppets

WHAT YOU NEED

- [ ] several paper cups
- [ ] crayons or felt-tipped marking pens
- [ ] a stapler and staples
- [ ] a pencil
- [ ] a pair of scissors
- [ ] cellophane or masking tape
- [ ] pieces of string or elastic
- [ ] brads and/or paper clips
- [ ] toothpicks and/or pipe cleaners
- [ ] an assortment of things from your odds and ends collection, including fabric scraps, ribbon, and yarn

WHAT YOU DO

1. Rinse and dry the cups.
2. Using your imagination and some things from your odds and ends collection, add the features that are needed—for example, eyes, noses, ears, mouths, arms, legs, and wings —to turn your cups into characters.

YOU CAN MAKE

Birds or Bats

Make a bird or a bat by drawing a face on your cup and adding wings. If you are making a bird, you may want to add a feather or two.

A Rabbit

Draw a rabbit's face on a paper cup. Add cloth or paper ears. For the body, dress your arm in a white sock. Glue felt or paper legs and a cotton puff tail to the sock.

Cup Puppets
(continued)

YOU CAN MAKE

Talking Puppets

To make a talking puppet, find two cups with handles. Stack the cups so that the tops are together and the handles are one below the other.

Fasten the cups together by running a strip of masking tape from one cup to the other between the open handles.

Use yarn, paper, and/or marking pens to add hair and facial features to the top cup. Then, fold the handles back and hold your puppet as shown.

Stacks of Acrobats

Glue or tape at least five cups together, top to top and bottom to bottom, to make a stack of acrobats. Add arms and legs made from paper or pipe cleaners. Use marking pens to draw hair and facial features, or cut them from paper or yarn and glue them on.

and Even a Monster

Turn a cup upside down, and add a crazy face. Staple a cloth body to the edge of the cup. Glue on paper strip legs. Use brads, paper clips, toothpicks, and other odds and ends to add antennae and special monstrous features.

Cup Puppet Patterns

noses

ears

mouths

eyes

Cup Puppet Patterns
(continued)

beaks

wings

legs

arms

Cup-and-Sock Puppets

WHAT YOU NEED

- [ ] a paper cup
- [ ] some felt-tipped marking pens
- [ ] a pair of scissors
- [ ] paper, felt, and/or fabric scraps
- [ ] white fabric glue
- [ ] an old sock
- [ ] a pencil, a pen, or some colored chalk
- [ ] a needle and thread (optional)
- [ ] an assortment of things from your odds and ends collection

WHAT YOU DO

1. Think about what kind of animal you will make and about how that animal looks. Are its ears long or short, large or small? Do they stand up on the animal's head, flop to the side, or lie flat? Are the animal's eyes large or small, round or oval? And what about the mouth?
2. Using the felt-tipped marking pens, draw the face of the animal you have decided to make on the cup.

Cup-and-Sock Puppets
(continued)

3. With shapes cut from paper, felt, or fabric scraps, add other features.

4. Set the cup head aside while you create the sock body.

5. Put the sock over your arm. Notice where the feet and tail should go, and mark these places lightly with a pencil, a pen, or some chalk.

6. Cut feet and a tail from paper, felt, or fabric.

7. Sew or glue these features to the sock.

8. Use pens, paper, felt, or fabric to add spots or stripes if you wish.

9. Put the sock on your arm. Put the cup over your hand—and there you have a cup-and-sock puppet!

10. Think of some words for your puppet to say, a story for it to tell, or a lesson for it to teach.

Paper Bag Rod Puppet: Head

WHAT YOU NEED

- [ ] a used paper lunch or grocery bag
- [ ] some newspapers
- [ ] a long cardboard tube
- [ ] a pair of scissors
- [ ] some glue
- [ ] masking tape
- [ ] crayons or felt-tipped marking pens
- [ ] construction paper in assorted colors
- [ ] crepe paper streamers or strips of colored paper
- [ ] feathers, felt, paper plates and cups (rinsed and dried for reusing), sticks, yarn, and other things from your odds and ends collection

WHAT YOU DO

1. Stuff the bag with newspapers.
2. Poke the cardboard tube into the bag to form the neck.
3. Squeeze the bag around the tube and use masking tape to fasten the bag securely around the tube.
4. With crayons or marking pens, draw a face on the bag.
5. Use some of your odds and ends to add a beak, a nose, ears, horns, and/or antlers.

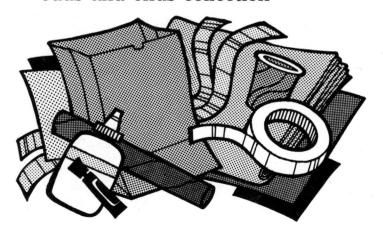

Paper Bag Rod Puppet: Head
(continued)

YOU CAN MAKE

a mouse

a lop-eared rabbit

an elephant

a buzzard

a lion

a bear

Paper Bag Rod Puppet: Body

After you have finished the head, make a body for your paper bag rod puppet.

WHAT YOU NEED

- ☐ a piece of cloth about 2 feet square
- ☐ a pair of scissors
- ☐ a piece of cardboard
- ☐ a pencil
- ☐ some glue
- ☐ a stapler and staples
- ☐ a thin dowel about 15 inches long
- ☐ masking tape

WHAT YOU DO

1. Fold the cloth in half.
2. With the scissors, cut a slit in the fold for the tube as shown.
3. To make hands for your puppet, place each of your hands on the cardboard and draw around it.
4. Carefully cut out the resulting mitten shapes and staple them inside the folded cloth.
5. Put the tube, or neck portion, of the puppet's head through the slit in the cloth.

Paper Bag Rod Puppet: Body
(continued)

6. Glue the edge of the cloth around the puppet's neck to hold it in place.
7. Tape the dowel to one of your puppet's hands.
8. To move your puppet, hold the tube in one hand and the dowel in the other.

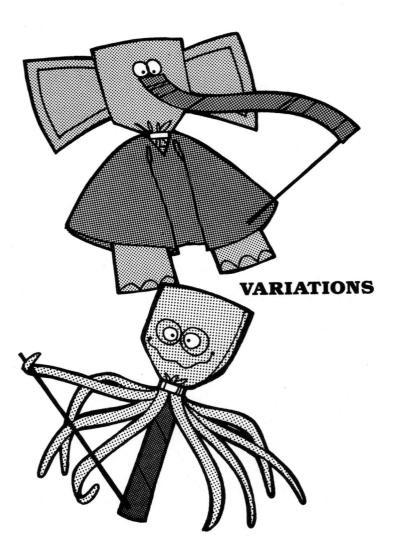

VARIATIONS

Paper Bag Vest

WHAT YOU NEED

- [ ] a large brown paper grocery bag
- [ ] a pencil
- [ ] a ruler
- [ ] a pair of scissors
- [ ] some glue
- [ ] crayons or felt-tipped marking pens
- [ ] leftover bits of construction paper, fabric, felt, rick-rack, wrapping paper, or other things from your odds and ends collection

WHAT YOU DO

1. Using the pencil and the ruler, draw a straight line up the middle of the front or back of the grocery bag.
2. Carefully cut along this line.
3. On the bottom of the bag, draw a circle large enough to go around your neck. Keep the circle small. Don't let it touch the edges of the bottom.
4. Cut out this circle.

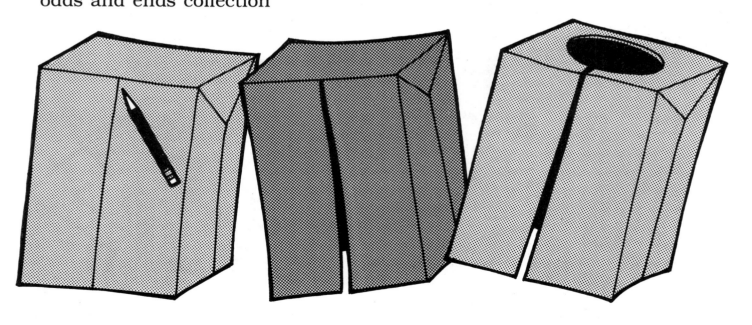

Paper Bag Vest
(continued)

5. Cut square holes in the sides for your arms.
6. Try on your vest and adjust the fit. If the vest is too long, trim the bottom to make it shorter. If the neck or armholes are too small, cut them to make them larger.

7. Fringe or scallop the bottom of the vest.
8. If there are words on your grocery bag, glue a piece of paper over them.
9. Decorate your vest. Draw on it with crayons or felt-tipped pens. Glue bits of paper, fabric, felt, or rick-rack to it.

Rock-and-Roll Egg Dolls

WHAT YOU NEED

- [ ] an empty egg-shaped panty hose package
- [ ] a small amount of salt, sand, or uncooked rice
- [ ] some masking tape
- [ ] permanent marking pens in a variety of colors
- [ ] self-adhesive dots, circles, and labels
- [ ] some stickers (optional)
- [ ] an assortment of things from your odds and ends collection, including braid, fabric, felt, lace, rick-rack, yarn, and scraps of construction paper
- [ ] a pair of sharp scissors
- [ ] some white glue

WHAT YOU DO

1. Open the egg and put some rice, salt, or sand in the bottom (wider) half.
2. Put the halves back together.
3. Wrap the seam with masking tape.
4. With the pens, some paper, felt or fabric scraps, and/or the self-adhesive dots, circles, and labels, create a face on the egg.
5. Using the stickers and the things from your odds and ends collection, add ears, a hat, some whiskers or a mustache, arms, feet, and maybe even a tail.